Listen, Management!

Listen, Management!

Creative Listening for Better Managing

WILLIAM F. KEEFE

McGRAW-HILL BOOK COMPANY

New York   St. Louis   San Francisco   Düsseldorf   Johannesburg
Kuala Lumpur   London   Mexico   Montreal   New Delhi
Panama   Rio de Janeiro   Singapore   Sydney   Toronto

Sponsoring Editors M. Joseph Dooher/ Dale L. Dutton
Director of Production Stephen J. Boldish
Editing Supervisors Barbara Church/ Carolyn Nagy
Designer Naomi Auerbach
Editing and Production Staff Gretlyn Blau,
 Teresa F. Leaden, George E. Oechsner

LISTEN, MANAGEMENT!

Copyright © 1971 by McGraw-Hill, Inc. All Rights Reserved. Printed in the United States of America. No part of this publication may be reproduced, stored in a retrieval system, or transmitted, in any form or by any means, electronic, mechanical, photocopying, recording, or otherwise, without the prior written permission of the publisher.

Library of Congress Catalog Card Number 78-134598

07-033436-6

1234567890 BPBP 754321

Preface

IMAGINE AN ORGANIZATION in which no one speaks. Ever. All communication is carried on by reading and writing—the written word.

Phantasmic? Unquestionably. And impossible. Meetings conducted in writing would be interminable and surface-scratching. The personnel officer who could not talk to a job candidate would end up tearing his hair. Desks without telephones, or without intercom buttons to connect those telephones to other parts of the organization, would look naked. The sales force that could not talk out its projects and problems would probably wither and die, its interest gone.

Gone would be the music of reasoned oral argument, verbal message sending and receiving of other kinds, the plea for faster action from Accounting, the face-to-face training sessions, the outbreaks of emotion in words, the shouted warning to the crane operator.

The silent dream does not and cannot exist. Within the organization we live, for better or worse, by neither the spoken nor the written word alone, but we use both in some kind of self-ordained proportion. And luckily, because no one, or only the very rare one, can say in writing what he will say orally if someone listens.

This is true in the literal sense: that the normal individual among us, including the manager and the executive, is incapable of putting into writing what he puts into speaking—all the thoughts, feelings, and facts, all the sensation and hidden meanings, all the humor and sense and sensibility that go into speech. For one person, even to attempt such rounded communication via the written word would be too embarrassing. For another, it might be too difficult, too time-consuming, too demanding, or too purposeless—so many things that we communicate verbally would rank as inconsequential if put on paper. Who will read this, and for what purpose? This is the type of question that would arise. Is it worth writing?

Our stricture is also true in a nonliteral sense. The oral phrasing always carries much more meaning than the same phrasing would when written out. The spoken word is freighted with more meaning because of voice tone, inflection, speed of delivery, accompanying movements and gestures, and other characteristics; and behind these, of course, the self that gives every man's words individuality and character. Two men may make essentially the same comment on the company's safety program—"It doesn't go far enough," for example. But they mean different things if we can learn those things.

Herein lies the best rationale for trying to listen professionally: to be able to sort out of verbal exchange those obvious or hidden, but unexpressed, items of information that give depth and clarity and deep focus to mere words: genuine understanding of the other and of what he is saying on the surface with his mouth and movements. Listening in this context becomes a purer form of interpersonal communication. It steps well beyond the physical excercise called hearing; we understand now what is meant by the statement, "Listening is with the mind, hearing with the senses." Listening is now seen as the means of bridging the gap between one mind and another, one interior person and another—a gap that may actually be widened by words where listening does not receive its meed of attention.

Listening is in the organization, as in life, to stay. It is there because oral communication is there to stay. So listen as if your life, your career in the organization, depended on it. It may. If this book helps impart some knowledge of the why's and how's, we've done our job.

ACKNOWLEDGMENTS

To A. A. IMBERMAN, who many years ago gave me my first opportunity to listen professionally;

To TIMOTHY J. HOLLAND, whose advice and suggestions on portions of the incomplete manuscript were invaluable;

To MY WIFE MOLLY, whose patience was monumental,

And to all the numerous others who gave moral support.

William F. Keefe

Contents

Preface v

1. Introduction: Listening for Managers, Executives — 1
2. Why Listen? — 23
3. The Listening Mind — 46
4. Creativity—the Element of Adventure — 68
5. Preparation—Mental, Emotional, and Physical — 90
6. The Fact and the Act of Listening — 110
7. Ingredients of the Method — 136
8. Listen When—and with Whom? Closing the Circle — 157
9. Pitfalls — 181

Index 193

Listen, Management!

1
Introduction: Listening for Managers, Executives

> Nature gave us two ears and only one mouth so that we could listen twice as much as we speak. —Proverb

COLOR HIM BRIGHT. He's the *man* of action and the *manager* of action in business and industry.

His characteristics are by now well known. To name a key one, he devotes little time to the nitty-gritty chorework of the organization. Rather, he appears to stand aside from that chorework and to influence and guide it.

This new-model man-manager stimulates, pushes, prods. He decides. He sets an organizational stage and then walks off when the action starts. He may set several stages; he may help launch the action on each. But basically he remains in the wings, making sure the actors are playing their roles well. The momentum of the action is as important to him as its goals and particular form and substance. He manages action to *be* the man of action.

His energy and attention seem inward-focused—directed within himself as much as toward the external facts of organizational life. His mind weighs what he is and what others are; and what little prods and pushes are required to keep the whole operation moving seem sometimes to come from him as second thoughts, or strokes of inspiration. He is, thus, both thoughtful and action-oriented: a paradox. He is also inspired in his decisions and enthusiasm yet cool in his assessments of possible alternatives.

Growth is this new man-manager's middle name—his own growth and that of the organization. And by growth is meant dynamic growth like that of a living organism: growth reaching into all the organization's corners.

In the view of modern management theorists, he is a communicator. He manages by communication. That means he is listener and speaker, communicator and communicated-to. But he is not equal parts listener and speaker. He knows the wisdom of the proverb, "Nature gave us two ears and only one mouth so that we could listen twice as much as we speak."

He is two parts listener and one part speaker to be supportive: to encourage and to obtain ideas. He seeks the truth of a situation and knows that the truth will die in a system of one-way communication. This man-manager employs his listening-communication powers to create the atmosphere in which the truths of a problem come quickly and easily to his attention.

He remains always aware that his listening contributes to the operational efficacy—even the mental health—of those around him in the organization. Just as the individual in private life needs someone to talk to, someone to listen to him, so does the individual in the organization. The functional effectiveness of the individual in either situation may—some authorities believe it does—hinge on exactly this: whether he feels that he is *listened to*.

In this new manager's dispensation listening is a kind of recognition of another as a person, and perhaps the most fundamental kind of recognition: perhaps much more fundamental than a note of commendation or a medal that gathers dust or a twenty-five-year watch.

And if this is true, the man-manager of action is always contributing to the working potential of the whole organization, or to his portion of it. If personal mental health is closely bound up with the need to have a listening ear, whether wife or husband, sweetheart, parent or child, the business organization benefits in like manner from listeners. Through listening the organization's problems find the channels where they will not only be recognized but attacked and solved.

This new breed of manager knows a whole school of psychotherapy employs listening as its chief tool. He has seen in our society, history's most communications-wise, how failure to listen has built huge gaps: generation gaps, race gaps, town and gown gaps and others, all of them productive of strife and turmoil.

This new manager, finally, has observed how men view their gods. He has recognized the basic truth that these gods derive their power and glory from the fact that men believe their gods will listen to them, that through prayer the lonely, lowly individual can gain divine help or intercession. On the mundane, man-made stage of the business organization the manager seeks to emulate these beneficent gods.

LISTENING: MEANING AND IMPORTANCE

Contract negotiations broke down. Suddenly, more than 25,000 employees of an automobile assembly plant in the Midwest "hit the bricks." They set up picket lines; they carried placards.

A newspaper reporter appeared on the scene. His assignment: to talk to some strikers, write a feature story on their reasons for striking. The reporter approached a placard-bearing striker and asked his question: "What are *your* reasons for being on strike?"

"Man," the striker said, "if you only knew. No one in there ever listens to us. So—we give them a strike."

In this true anecdote a man spoke unscientifically of listening. Seeing an absence of listening he sensed disparagement of his dignity and humanity.

What is listening? Can we define it? It does not mean "to do what the speaker wants," or merely to stand attentive, though the word has acquired those colloquial connotations.

No. For our purposes it relates first to the listener, secondly to the person listened to. In the business context it can be defined as *the conscious, active process of eliciting information, ideas, attitudes, and emotions in interpersonal, oral exchange for the purpose of increasing the listener's capacity for planning and decision making.*

The manager employs up-listening in reference to his superiors, lateral-listening in reference to his equals, and down-listening in reference to his subordinates. In our study we will emphasize down-listening simply because most errors, and those often the most costly to the organization, occur in superior-subordinate communication, or lack of it. Beyond that, of course, the manager *is* a manager most essentially in relation to those under him. If he has no subordinates, he is a general without an army and will be more order taker than manager.

The Minisociety

The costs of poor or no listening, because they can run as high as the very survival of the organization, point up the enormity of the challenge facing the busy manager or executive.

This executive or manager is surrounded by experts who advise, assist, devise, develop, and execute; by middle experts, middle and lower management people, down to supervisors and line foremen; and, on the lowest rungs of the ladder, the doers in production—the workers—the men and women who run machines, assemble, move and ship, type and file, and keep records.

The various groupings form the typical, complex minisociety known as The Organization. All contain more or fewer individuals who have been fitted into organizational niches to do specific jobs. Each individual serves as an extension of top management's mind and will.

The managerial challenge is to direct and control them, to influence and motivate them, even though each individual among them has a mind and a will of his own, even though each may stand two or three, or five or six, hierarchical removes from the source of authority and influence. They act, at every level, just as does the executive: for reasons that they understand clearly, dimly, or not at all.

Through communication, the task of directing, controlling, influencing, and motivating—the task of managing—becomes functional. The modern business organization *must* churn to the rhythm of an unceasing, orchestrated flow of communication. External factors being equal, or at least normal, this organization's degree of success may hang entirely on how highly it orchestrates that flow.

Everyone Communicates: Few Do It Right

One truism is: no organization's members can function together without communicating. Another: few communicate in such a way as to give their communication the greatest effect.

Why? Partly because few in the typical organization *have* to do it right. Tom, at his double-end lathe, may go through an entire day without uttering a complete sentence. Mike, the foreman, may face only slightly greater need to communicate. He may find it hard to make himself heard above the machine roar of the mill, and use only sign language.

Not so with the manager or executive. He has graduated. He has left the ranks of those for whom communication can be part-time or primitive. He has the task, within his sphere of command, of orchestrating—of gearing his up, down, and lateral message sending and receiving and that of those around him and below him to obtain the highest performance dividends possible.

He has a monkey on his back. At our point in time the chances are that he is not aware of the need to communicate well.

Our downward-communications age This manager or executive lives in a society that prides itself on the power and multiplicity of the downward-communications devices and techniques that it makes available. He performs in an Orwellian environment in which, as a manager, he can command a hundred different media from electronic bulletin boards and canned speeches to filmstrips and motion pictures. A magazine of audio-visual communications lists more than two dozen different, commonly used media in the AV field alone. A study of the most widely used methods of written and oral communication in business and industry names a hundred different techniques. Only a tiny handful leave room for audience participation or upward communication through question-answer or in other ways.

Leave the organization. Go beyond its walls. The quantity and diversity of the messages flowing in, without surcease, dazzle the eye and boggle the mind. The messages come from radio, television, newspapers. From magazines and special interest publications of all kinds.

No one can possibly absorb it all. Outside the office, in consequence, the manager or executive, like everyone else, must listen with incredibly heightened selectivity or not at all. He must listen selectively in self-defense.

With what result? With the result that we have become conditioned to think outward, downward, one-way communication simply because that is what we are primarily exposed to. We tune out. To avoid becoming victims of overcommunication, too many of us develop the "positive art of not listening." But in tuning out we are *becoming victims* in the sense that we assume nonlistening to be a normal principle of communication. "Americans are not good listeners. In general they talk more than they listen. Competition in our culture has put a premium on self-expression, even if the individual has nothing to express." [1]

Two authorities speak Still more underlies the modern phenomenon of nonlistening.

"Early childhood has been concentrated on reading and

---

[1] Stuart Chase, "Are You Listening?" *Readers' Digest*, December, 1962, p. 83.

writing . . . ," wrote Walter S. Wilstrom of the National Industrial Conference Board. "The school program, with its many opportunities for youngsters to speak and make formal reports, has provided much practice in speaking. . . . On the other hand, it has usually been assumed that children know how to hear everything that is said to them." [2]

In other words, we are "educationally deprived" as far as listening is concerned. "For the improvement of personal communication our school curriculums have been seriously out of balance. The eye has occupied the favored position, with the visual skills of reading and writing getting chief attention. Meanwhile, the aural skills of speaking and listening have been kept in the background. . . ." [3]

In aping our downward-communications environment, in submitting to the communications imbalance of our educational system, we have become a performing, talking, public speaking, nonlistening race. For society, the results are the yawning communications gaps already mentioned. For business and industry the results can be summarized in a word: waste. American managements, noted a top executive of a major corporation, have spent a billion dollars a year since the middle 1950s in communicating with employees. Most of this effort has brought "a sea of words, an avalanche of paper, a babel of noise, and a pitifully small return on the investment."

That waste is the dividend of what *Newsweek* once called the "billion-dollar employee communications programs" is difficult to question. The mass media still shout their news of strikes, walkouts, sitdowns, lockouts; of firms where people-generated problems from low productivity to unconscionable turnover run rampant. No one seemed surprised that unionized work units in the middle and latter 1960s began rejecting at an unprecedented clip the contracts that union-manage-

[2] Walter S. Wikstrom, "Lessons in Listening," *The Conference Board Record*, The National Industrial Conference Board Inc., New York, April, 1965, p. 17.

[3] Ralph G. Nichols and Leonard A. Stevens, *Are You Listening?* McGraw-Hill Book Company, New York, 1957, p. 7.

ment negotiating teams had worked out with the aid of federal mediation authorities. Those contracts were being rejected at the rate of one in seven in 1967, or 14.8 percent, as contrasted with 8.7 percent in 1964. The rate will undoubtedly see rises and falls, but could easily continue into and through the 1970s at epidemic level.

What workers are saying when they vote down contracts should be clear. They are saying to union and management, "A plague on both your houses." And this in face of the billions of dollars American industry spends on downward-communications. In the process of generating those communications, too many have forgotten that "Listening to employees, trying sincerely to get their interpretations and ideas, and acting on the basis of what they think, not what we think, or what we wish they could think, is absolutely essential to realistic management." [4]

F. J. Roethlisberger, an early authority on listening, noted the connection between failure to listen and labor strife years ago. "Have we not (here) a clue as to the possible basis for labor unrest and disputes? Granted that . . . disputes are often stated in terms of wages, hours of work, and physical conditions of work, is it not possible that these demands are disguising, or in part are the symptomatic expression of, much more deeply rooted human situations which we have not as yet learned to recognize, to understand, and to control?" [5]

In other words, are workers not translating for management? Are they not saying, "These are the only things you know how to listen to?" Or: "Because you cannot master our two-way language in the workplace, we will speak your one-way language at the negotiating table."

As far as the more interpersonal communications skills, speaking and listening, are concerned, managers and executives have been walking on one leg. One skill, listening, has been largely ignored. This has thrown their whole communi-

[4] Denis Murphy, *Better Business Communication*, McGraw-Hill Book Company, New York, 1957, p. 155.
[5] F. J. Roethlisberger, *Management and Morale*, Harvard University Press, Cambridge, Mass., 1955, p. 25.

cations orientation off balance. Some inadequate substitutes for skilled interpersonal listening have been hurled into the breach: attitude surveys, for example, and suggestion systems. But these cannot supplant a communication skill that should be functioning for the manager during all his working hours.

Proof from statistics We can approach the question of the importance of listening statistically. We can make a start by asking and answering two questions:

- What percentage of their time on the job do managers and executives spend in communicating?
- What percentage of that communicating time do managers and executives spend in listening?

Executives themselves answer the first question. "I spend at least 90 percent of my time on the job communicating with people," notes the top executive of a major American corporation. Ten other high executives who were asked for their estimates for this study placed their communication time at 70 to 100 percent of their working time.

Granted that executives below the top level, and in smaller companies perhaps some at the top, spend less time communicating and more time doing or directly handling operational matters. It remains true that the percentage of time spent communicating represents far and away the bulk of the executive's or manager's time. One authority, George S. Odiorne, author of the book *How Managers Make Things Happen,* estimates that *managers and line supervisors* spend 1,200 to 1,500 hours a year meeting and talking to people—communicating with them—including listening as part of that function.

If the "normal" work year comprises anywhere from 1,800 to 2,400 hours, line supervisors and managers spend from 55 to more than 80 percent of their working time in communicating. The manager-executive, in the nature of things, spends more. He is more communicator, planner and decider, less the operational doer.

What of the second question? A survey taken by Paul T. Rankin in 1929 has direct pertinence. Rankin found that the sixty-eight adults taking part in the survey spent 9 percent of their communication time in writing, 16 percent of their time reading, 30 percent talking and 45 percent listening. The participants kept records on the time spent on the four phases of communication through a series of working days.

Equally interesting are figures cited by Nichols and Stevens. The authors refer to a survey taken by the American Dietetic Association of 110 dieticians in various parts of the country. These are the averaged figures showing how the survey participants spent their *communicating* time:

```
Reading  . . . . . .  4 percent
Writing  . . . . . . 11 percent
Speaking . . . . . . 22 percent
Listening. . . . . . 63 percent [6]
```

From these surveys we can deduce, with Wikstrom, that managers and executives spend 45 to 63 percent of their communication time on the job at *listening*.

The evidence suggests that the typical business and industrial organization is paying its managers and executives primarily to communicate just to manage. But company after company is not getting its money's worth.

Where listening isn't practiced The substantive, negative effects of poor communication stemming from failure to listen go much more deeply into the fiber and fabric of an organization than any figures could show.

Management has been defined as "the art of getting things done through people." But as J. C. Penney once noted, "the art of effective listening is essential to clear communication, and clear communication is necessary to management success."[7] In other words, you cannot "get things done through people" without listening.

Since management goes on even where listening is not practiced, some major dangers rear their heads. To name the key ones:

[6] Nichols and Stevens, *op. cit.*, p. 8.
[7] J. C. Penney, "What an Executive Should Know About Himself," The Dartnell Corporation, Chicago, Ill., 1964, p. 23.

■ Management may talk past, or act without knowledge of, the true facts and issues and thus defeat its own purposes.

Acting without adequate information and understanding, the management running afoul of this danger often fills its publications with material of little or no real interest to employees. Typically, a 1947 Opinion Research Corporation survey showed that the president's letter praising free enterprise in one company publication ranked ninety-seventh among ninety-seven items considered. Years ago, *Fortune* magazine asked, "Is Anybody Listening?" (to company pronouncements) —and answered in the negative. On the operational side, an uninformed management may launch program after program, see the project or program fail, and switch suddenly to an alternative course of action. It may become a laughingstock in the eyes of employees. "Another big crusade that'll blow over in six months," sigh the line supervisors in such firms.

■ Management may project its communications/human relations approach through people who can only handicap its operation.

This danger arises because good communication goes hand in hand with good human relations. The top management working without good listening risks having neither; often, it does not or cannot decide what type of people should represent it on the lower rungs. The danger often finds expression in what has been called the "John Syndrome."

> John managed a department in a plant manufacturing office equipment. He stayed in his job because he had once done a personal service for the president of the firm. With his men, however, he rated as a "bull of the woods." He never listened to them. The complete autocrat, he practiced what Rensis Likert has called the "exploitive-authoritative" style of managing. Everyone at or near the top found a way to excuse him: "That's old John," they said, ignoring the indices of poor performance in John's department. Under John, the department's turnover had long since passed the limits of the expectable. Men at every level were requesting transfers. Productivity was low.
>
> Eventually, even the president came to see that John was se-

riously handicapping the entire company. Every sample of poor supervision or bad management in any department could be rationalized as being "not as bad as John's department." John was finally put on the shelf, in a job without direct supervisory responsibility. Things in his department began to pick up.

■ In talking down or out, and not receiving up through listening, management may become so introverted that its decision-making powers wither away.

Any business organization may encounter this danger. Too many poor decisions rob management of its confidence, or unrealistic policies fail, making management lose its verve and daring—if it ever had any.

> A family-owned bakery employing some 400 workers operated pretty much "by the seat of its pants." No one in management listened; policies and decisions were made on the spot and without regard to the consequences. Often, two orders contradicted one another. Members of the family joined the firm whenever they needed jobs: round pegs in square holes. As time passed, the day-to-day chores of running the business were taken care of; but management postponed long-range decisions, or took too long in making them, with the result that opportunities passed, never to appear again. The decisions that did emerge from the inner councils often fell flat. No one could dispose or decide effectively because no one else was listening.

■ Management may communicate for communication's sake, and not to reach a person or group with a meaningful message.

The management in this position makes communication an end in itself; it counts the quantity and diversity of its communications devices and forgets the goals of communication. This management may even set itself targets: three bulletin board notices a week, or one letter to employees' homes every month. Too often "meeting the target" becomes more important than transmitting valid and valuable information. A formula may key an entire communications policy: "We will stop talking about the 'three B's'—Brides, Babies, and Bowling—and talk about the 'three P's' of Productivity, Profits, and Principles." But the body still lacks warmth, heart.

- With authority flowing out or down and no or too little ideation or information flowing in and up, the voices of the future grow silent.

In this situation management slowly strangles those more creative, thoughtful souls who could be its salvation. Since good people cannot make themselves heard, or their weight felt, they retaliate with indifference. A yawn greets the new sales program. Orders fall into a vacuum of disinterest. The best men leave. Deprived of the divergent, concerned views that listening could deliver to it, management finds itself planning poorly for the future.

- Finally, where authority functions in an atmosphere of inadequate upward communication, it may actually arouse resistance to its orders and decrees.

How this happens has been documented in case after case. Management decides on a far-reaching machine replacement program, but because it has not read the situation closely through listening or has not prepared the psychological ground for the change, it finds its work force, or even its management staff, fighting the innovation tooth and nail. What should have been hailed as improvement contributing to the overall health of the organization becomes the grist of bitter argument. Two things are normally happening in such situations:

1. Management fails to answer or settle the questions, hesitations, doubts, and second thoughts that it must answer before introducing change; it does not do so because it cannot—it has no deep, accurate awareness of such doubts and questions.

2. Management is not recognizing the reality that formal authority may be more nominal than real authority unless and until it is accepted by those subject to it. Such acceptance presupposes understanding of management's goals and intentions in exercising authority. Again, management cannot transmit such understanding without knowing through listening whether and where understanding gaps exist.

Most tragically, perhaps, "unlistening" or nonlistening companies or individuals defend themselves. "We're surviving," they state. They might as well argue that modern communications devices are irrelevant because no one used them a hundred years ago.

The nonleader Nonlistening, learned typically in the school years, receives reinforcement when the individual moves out into the world. At this point, as an adult, the individual is exposed to the suffocating overcommunication of our time. If he enters an organization where nonlistening is the rule, he normally adjusts to his new environment; the organizational milieu becomes a third powerful force encouraging nonlistening. Eventually the nonlistener may become the nonleader.

Not all in this situation see themselves for what they are. Many believe themselves to be good listeners. But they cannot back up their laudatory self-analysis. The Opinion Research Corporation of Princeton, New Jersey, carried out a survey in four large companies. The findings showed that 77 percent of the supervisors interviewed felt themselves to be good listeners. Other data gave them the lie.

Both supervisors and other management staff members were asked to list those factors that, in their opinion, nonsupervisory employees considered most important. Their choices varied substantially from the factors listed by the employees themselves. Supervisors seriously underestimated employees' desire for good working conditions. Supervisors and others also undervalued their subordinates' need to work with congenial fellows and to get along with others around them.

Case histories make the same point. A management burdened with nonleadership is told that a strike is imminent; it laughs off the report, saying, "We've never had a strike here," and is shocked when its workers walk out. Another management receives clear warning that one of its top researchers is about to leave; nothing is done and the man leaves, crippling a whole operation.

This is unleadership or nonleadership through nonlistening, and its effects range through the catalog of organizational indices of performance. They include turnover ratios, productivity, grievance rates, absenteeism figures, P and L statements, safety records, and so on. Very typically, in organizations suffering from this sickness, negative group moods, attitudes, and policies develop. Many of them become sloganized:

"Let George do it."

"Don't rock the boat."

"I'm not going to stick *my* neck out."

And so on. The slogans, each representing a philosophy of below-the-top management, in nearly all cases bespeak nonleadership. They express what has been called "anomie," the alienation that digs a gap between what managements want of their members and what they are willing to give.

Make no bones about it: What is thought and done, what *happens,* below the top ranges of the organization is almost always found on investigation to be the echo of how communication and the exercise of authority are practiced at the top. One poor communicator, one nonleader in a seat of authority, can cause any or all of those effects of nonleadership such as high turnover and high grievance rates. This nonleader can do more.

> In a 300-man department in a chemical plant the assistant department manager had made himself notorious because of his "exploitive-authoritative" approach. After a three-week strike, management went seeking the real reasons why workers had "gone out." During the investigation the assistant manager's name turned up repeatedly. Management finally put together a picture showing that this one man had produced such violently anticompany attitudes in his department that the department's workers had evangelized for a strike to "get even." They had succeeded despite management's offer of an excellent new contract.

Nonlistening *cum* nonleadership can have less serious consequences, of course. A nonlistening management may simply not have the interest, ability or awareness needed to communicate the fact that it is doing a job. It may be unable to get employees "thinking company." Often an anomalous situation arises.

> The superintendent of a steel fabricating plant in the East did not want to learn to communicate. He ignored bulletin boards,

refused to authorize a plant paper. He never gave a talk to employees, and avoided other opportunities to inform them on matters of general interest. He didn't believe any of these things necessary. The plant paid good wages and had every conceivable employee benefit. It even offered free income tax assistance at the appropriate time of the year. In an operational sense the plant seemed to run well enough. Yet absenteeism ran far above the average for the area or industry. Occasionally the workers in one department or another would walk out—in defiance of the company and their own union officials. Labor unrest and poor morale showed themselves in many other ways; scrap rates ran high, for example. These problems cost the company huge sums.

This is managerial blindness. It occurs in every industry. It stems from a refusal to acknowledge the importance of communication including listening. Such cases suggest that to give benefits without communicating information, goals, and challenges, without making adjustments based on knowledge gained through listening, may be wasting well-intentioned effort. Hell is paved with unanswered questions about benefits and policies.

The nonlistener faces one other ever-present problem. Not knowing his people and being inadequately informed, he may veer sharply from one side to another, from one approach to another. His managerial needle may swing wildly, leaving confusion, fear, or insecurity, behind. Once the manager's subordinates no longer know what they can expect of or from him, they tread warily. His archetype is the executive who told everyone that "my door is open" and then harshly reprimanded a subordinate who brought in an idea without going through channels.

PERSONALITY, STYLE, AND LISTENING

Turn now to a seeming paradox. Personality determines a manager's style and the manager's style tells how he will listen. Personality remains basically constant, but style can be changed and listening can be learned. Where it is learned, it becomes the element that gives life to an obsolete or ineffective style.

"How?" The answer is growth.

"Know thyself," said the ancient Greeks. The phrase suggests that with true self-knowledge an individual can adjust his inner realities, his flaws and strengths, his ambitions and attitudes, to the outer realities of the world. He sees himself in perspective.

"Knowing yourself" as a manager, you can see your working style, whatever it may be, as the collective expression of your on-the-job personality. You will be able correctly to assess your capacity for learning. You will find that capacity, if at all substantial, to be the open sesame to expansion of style and philosophy to include broader and more productive communication skills, including listening. The road to such self-development has three main bends, all of them negotiable:

- Establishment of a healthy mental and emotional attitude toward communication in general and listening in particular
- Acquisition of knowledge of the techniques or tools of listening
- Persistent application of the techniques or tools

You can learn listening, in short, as you learned golf. You can learn it even if your job environment discourages it: you need not necessarily and inevitably succumb, the victim of your surroundings. Just as nearly every organization of any size has its ultra-authoritative "John," so most organizations, no matter how inept at communication, have their beacon in the wilderness: the one good listener who redeems the organization's or a department's faith in the company.

The conscientious manager seeks to move his world, his part of the organization: he wants to manage. He does not deceive himself with the thought that he, and he alone, can produce all the ideas that will help perform that moving job. He welcomes others' ideas; he works for better communication of every type. He knows that "all the communication skills . . . appear to be elements of leadership, and the degree to which they are mastered is often a good measure of supervisory competence."[8]

Everyone operates differently Then listening stands as a reality-oriented goal worth working toward according to your own method and at your own speed. No one should be embarrassed if he takes a different road from that chosen by another manager or executive. Everyone operates differently.

> Executive Smith serves as vice-president, manufacturing, of a firm producing heating equipment. Smith decided years ago to learn to listen well. He tells of his appointment as manager of a key department. He had a lot to learn; he went about learning it with all dispatch. He soon received feedback indicating that his production workers regarded him as a "cold fish."
>
> Smith set about revising the general impression workers had of him. Without making a federal case of it, he slowed down the merest fraction in his circuits of the department. He listened. He took time to say hello; he learned names. He stopped to ask questions of a foreman, and often brought the hourly hands into consideration of a problem. Within weeks Smith began receiving a different kind of feedback: the men were changing their original impression.
>
> Smith built from there. He developed a natural sensitivity and an instinct for empathizing with people into a style of communicating that became, in effect, his style of managing.

Was this man unique? Yes, in the sense that he had his own self-made, instinctive style. No, not in the sense that he was the only man who ever mastered listening under his own power. Many have done it. Smith simply made up his mind to remove the "filter" of which authorities on communication have so often spoken. That filter sorts and classifies, rejecting many ideas that might have contributed to understanding.

---

[8] Charles E. Redfield, *Communication in Management*, The University of Chicago Press, Chicago, Ill., p. 169. Copyright 1953 by The University of Chicago. All rights reserved. Published 1953. Second impression 1954. Composed and printed by The University of Chicago Press, Chicago, Illinois, U.S.A.

The filter is built upon and maintained—or removed if the listener so wills—by attitude.

We can control and change our attitudes. They should, in fact, be adjusted continually to take account of new problems and circumstances. Of new challenges. Every manager should take such control and make such changes in his own way. Then he can grow.

Don't misconceive listening "I don't want to learn to listen," the manager of a plastics plant once told me. "I'm trying to get my people to listen to *me.*"

This man labored under a misconception. He felt listening would weaken his position and steal some of the authoritative zing from his decisions and orders. Listening, he thought, might even square with a type of surrender, a namby-pamby, wishy-washy management style. A highly intelligent and cultured man, he had a poor track record in his multiplant company: labor unrest followed him wherever he managed. Yet *that* he wrote off airily as "the breaks of the game."

He never, to my knowledge, came to see that listening held the key to the problem of "getting my people to listen to me." "Others will do to you as you do to them"—this might be the controlling rubric here.

Authority after authority has taken cognizance of this fact as far as managing is concerned. "Participative management" (management based in listening) has repeatedly been described as action-oriented management that neither implies managerial passivity nor excuses a failure to lead. On the contrary, it calls for decisive action on the basis of wide contribution of ideas—where this is appropriate.

McGregor notes in this regard:

> Acceptance of Theory Y (supportive or participative management, as contrasted with Theory X, authoritarian management) does not imply abdiction, or "soft" management, or "permissiveness." Such notions stem from the acceptance of authority as the *single* means of managerial control. . . . Theory Y assumes that people will exercise self-direction and self-control in the

achievement of organizational objectives to the degree that they are committed to those objectives.[9]

"Listening makes listeners," in the words of Nichols-Stevens. It also makes doers; it seeks to obtain commitment, action. The Listener in business is the one who really gets things done.

Herein lies the crucial importance of listening as a managerial skill. It seeks to obtain the greatest possible degree of commitment. The manager who decides to learn listening may, of course, have to subject himself to an agonizing reassessment. Assume, for the sake of simplicity, that the three most widely inclusive styles of management are what they are so often held to be:

Free-rein
Democratic
Autocratic

The manager practicing the third style may have to throw out entirely some of the harsher characteristics of his managerial method. If he often rides roughshod over people without regard to their feelings, ideas, attitudes, or human dignity, he may find listening difficult at the start. The reason: Listening is doing the reverse of what has been second nature to him; it accords weight and meaning to others' thoughts and feelings.

The manager practicing listening inclines toward "democratic" management, that middle-of-the-road style characterized by a willingness to bring subordinates into his planning, creating, decision-making processes. But he does not climb into a stylistic straitjacket or even, necessarily, develop a wholly new style. He must develop and retain his own style or he will not be comfortable.

Can listening be dysfunctional for the manager practicing it? Can it hinder, not help, in the pursuit of more excellent performance? If it does, it has been misconceived and is being misused. It should lend depth to thinking, breadth to evi-

[9] Douglas McGregor, *The Human Side of Enterprise*, McGraw-Hill Book Company. New York, 1960, p. 56.

dence gathering, validity to decision making. The kind of listening we will be describing should *give* confidence and assuredness, not take it away.

The manager learning listening as an art will be trying to "get his dollar's worth" out of that considerable amount of communication time that he spends in listening under any circumstances.

LISTENING AND THE EXECUTIVE'S PERSONAL COMMUNICATION SKILLS INVENTORY

Communication, then, ranks as the executive's or manager's main task if he is actually to manage, to lead. On both statistical and practical grounds, listening ranks number one among the four basic communications skills of reading, writing, speaking, and listening.

To set the record straight we must now place listening in the number one spot on an emphasis basis. To bring his communication skills into true balance the manager or executive must give listening primary emphasis.

A chart for self-development, issued by one company for the guidance of its managers, suggests why.

> Managing is a distinct and professional kind of work, namely, leading by persuasion rather than by command: through planning, organizing, integrating and measuring; in the balanced and effective use of all the human and material resources of the enterprise . . . ; acting with initiative, self-development, self-discipline, and competence as to . . . personal work, voluntary teamwork and *two-way communication;* to accomplish desired performance and results. [Italics mine.]

Listening makes interpersonal communication two-way. The listener leads; he gets things done through others. Listening is the other half of talking. "And yet it is the listening and not the talking that produces the better results." [10] And listening

[10] Wouter van Garrett, "Do You Ever Stop to Listen?" *The American Mercury,* November, 1956, p. 143.

can be learned by anyone with common sense—*if* he will work at it. Like any other communication skill, listening takes hard work. It takes as much work, in its own way, as management itself. It has been called an acquired art. The manager willing to invest that mountain of enterprise and initiative required to learn good management should also be willing to develop this one skill, listening, that rounds off—sets off—his other skills. In so doing he can approach that plateau of finesse and expertness summed up in an associate's description of industrialist Charles Schwab: "Listening with him is an instinct as well as a rare charm. Whoever talks to him, be he day laborer or financier, faces a man who harkens gravely, attentive, eye to eye, until the speaker is quite done."

Schwab knew the golden rule of listening: listen unto others as you would have others listen unto you.

2
Why Listen?

> The World Should Listen Then—As I Am Listening Now. —P.B. SHELLEY

"I SIT HERE ALL DAY trying to persuade people to do the things they ought to have sense enough to do without my persuading them," said Harry S. Truman, thirty-third President of the United States.

Truman referred to his decision-making power in relation to his communication function. As chief executive of the world's most powerful nation, he saw his most basic function as the communication of decision in such a way that something happens.

The manager or executive in business and industry stands in different, nongovernmental shoes. But he has fundamentally the same function: to persuade others to *do*. He seeks to help harness the human energies of his organization, or of his portion of it, and to "hitch those energies to a common cause."

He does it best through skilled communication rooted firmly in expert listening.

THE GOALS ARE THE SAME AS FOR GOOD MANAGEMENT ITSELF

The cries sound plaintive. "I can't listen." "I don't have time to listen.' They reveal, first, inadequate comprehension of what listening involves and, second, lack of understanding of the reasons for listening: its purposes and goals. No one can afford *not* to listen any more than he can afford not to grow, to learn.

What does good listening involve? In terms of time, it adds little or nothing to the typical manager's work load. Genuine, skilled listening is marked more by highly developed technique than by additional input of time, more by professionalization of technique than by broadened effort. Higher quality, rather than greater quantity, is the goal.

We are suggesting that the manager learn listening, in sum, to know what he is doing as he communicates. The listening manager prepares and uses his mind according to basic principles. He continues to use his ears as transmission devices, but he engages his mind more and more as an analytic machine. He decodes as messages come in; he sorts and catalogues. Here listening differentiates itself from mere *hearing:* hearing may be described as mechanical while listening is largely mental.

Initially, of course, the manager going into listening to learn may invest more time in practice. He would do the same if he were learning golf, riflery, cost accounting, or French. The learning listener may seek out more opportunities for listening; he may broaden the range of his listening to include many who earlier stood along the wayside of his communication road. But while listening to any given individual he will typically spend no more time than before, when he listened unprofessionally. Eventually he may spend less time as he winnows more skillfully the valuable information from the valueless.

What of the goals of listening? They are the goals of good management everywhere. Listening aims at improvement of management skills in the communication area, and through that at better management. It *must* have this aim because most essentially "management is people," and the manager reaches and influences people through communication. Going a step farther, let us suppose "that he (the manager or executive) is interested in the same objectives that most modern managers seek to attain when they can shift their attention from the pressure of immediate assignments." Five generally accepted goals are listed:

"1. To raise the level of employee motivation

2. To increase the readiness of subordinates to accept change

3. To improve the quality of all managerial decisions

4. To develop teamwork and morale

5. To further the individual development of employees"[1]

The listening of which we write has these general goals.

More Specifically: The Goals

William Foote Whyte has called listening *action research*. The term, while employed by Whyte in reference to a consultant's listening, helps illuminate another aspect of its purposive function in the hands, or head, of the listening manager or executive.

Listening's *action* and *research* aspects complement one another. Listening has an *action* element because its performance produces the beneficial effects established as end-goals of its research aspect: it encourages others to talk, to make idea contributions. In listening the manager brings another into his councils and in following through on what is heard he effects action or change or adjustment. The other, the listenee, thus has helped make action, plan or change and is committed to it. But listening is also *research* because it seeks useful infor-

---

[1] Robert H. Tannenbaum and Warren H. Schmidt, "How to Choose a Leadership Pattern," *Harvard Business Review*, vol. 36, pp. 95–101, 1958.

mation and guidance that enables the listener to gear his decisions to realities in the environment.

For just a moment, watch an expert listener in action. The manager of an industrial plastics plant, he recently concluded a series of "where we stand" talks to employees of his 2,000-man plant. The talks were delivered before groups of forty to one hundred employees; the plant manager took two weeks to give all the talks. Now he is touring the plant in search of firsthand feedback.

Many workers know him, of course. They have heard his talks semiannually for two years. They nod or wave, or talk to him, as he passes with his personnel relations director. He spends a few seconds to a couple of minutes with each of forty or fifty men—foremen and workers both—while making his rounds. The plant manager makes notes as he goes; when he returns to his office he organizes his notes carefully. He has heard more than a dozen comments on his talks. From these he knows that the talks were widely accepted; he knows also that he can stress certain types of information a little more next time out. But from his notes he can also itemize literally dozens of ideas and suggestions on different levels of organizational significance. To name only a few:

■ *On the level of machine operations, safety, housekeeping, and other physical conditions:*

The distribution of space in the shipping department could be studied and, possibly, improved.

Water and oil drops from a floor above onto workers in one department.

A new drying system in grinding would help workers there meet production targets.

■ *On the level of plant facilities, methods and systems, and so on:*

Faster maintenance service would be appreciated in two departments.

People who have to handle the new order forms would appreciate some briefing on correct use of the forms.

■ *On the level of company benefits, special programs, communications, and training:*

Are new pension plan booklets coming soon to explain changes in the plan?

Will the plant paper have news on parking lot changes?
- *On the level of company or plant policy:*
Rotation of foremen among departments might be beneficial.

Can we set up uniform policies on absenteeism and tardiness?

The plant manager analyzed his notes with his personnel relations director. He made a couple of telephone calls. He wrote some notes to top aides, asking them to check out with the appropriate middle management personnel and foremen some of the questions he culled from his notes. In no case did he either reject out-of-hand a suggestion or idea, or assume without investigation that what he had heard was absolutely, factually true —except, of course, where he could verify a statement on the spot. He was taking action in both listening and following through; he was researching as well—gathering facts and ideas on one level, assessing mood and temper on another, listening for evidence pointing to future needs on a third.

With this actual case in front of us, we can look at the positive goals of listening from three different points of view:
1. In a project sense
2. In an organizational sense
3. In a personal development sense

In a Project Sense

First of all, listening seeks to produce information or evidence and more broadly based knowledge in reference to specific projects, tasks or plans. The plant manager in our case history completed his "plant walk" a wiser man. He knew what his communication project, the "where we stand" talks, had accomplished. He had discovered data pertinent to many other projects. He knew, for example, that a capital budget request had been entered for funds to expand Shipping-Receiving. On the basis of comments from production workers and foremen he could see in advance that expansion alone might be inadequate to satisfy what members of the department saw as needs; he asked that a thorough study be carried out to determine whether a complete physical realignment of the department would be called for—in conjunction with expansion.

Second, listening aims at achievement of at least some degree of participation; it proceeds from acceptance of the principle that others can and should contribute both *feed-in* before a project leaves the ground and *feedback* once it has been launched. The "others" may be workers, supervisors, managers, executives—depending on the situation. Depending on the problem or project, the participation may be formal or informal, broadly based or narrow. But listening in reference to a project or task or program requires acceptance that the other or others can contribute validly.

We should not misunderstand participation. It cannot be universal: neither workers nor a manager's immediate subordinates can take part in the formulation of every managerial decision. "Critics often misunderstand the use of participatory methods (of managing and making decisions). There is a place for management decision, and there is a place for sharing decision. The skillful manager will be able to integrate both procedures." [2]

Third, listening aims at motivating an employee or employees, no matter what their titles or job descriptions, to perform their best on the given assignment or project.

"Motivate or abdicate" might be the sloganized phrase summing up this phase of the manager's challenge. Listening has the positive goal of furnishing a concrete, psychologically valid, feasible way to meet that challenge. It permits others to contribute, to talk, on the theory that the man who talks is the one you can reach with motivation. "Who's in the best position to spot a better way to do a job?" asked the house organ of a major food manufacturer. "Usually the person closest to the job. . . . No wonder then that some of our best ideas for moving more products come from the men at the moving spot —our salesmen."

The paper added that the sales of one item doubled because the salesmen *saw their ideas going into effect*. Sales of other

---

[2] Alfred J. Marrow, *Making Management Human*, McGraw-Hill Book Company, New York, 1957, p. 192.

items increased perceptibly. The salesmen were motivated because what they suggested was accepted.

Fourth, listening in a project sense works pragmatically to produce ideas that have real value in the development or prosecution of the project or plan.

Listening has this concrete goal as well as the more abstract ones already listed. It hunts creativity. It seeks improvement. It tries to avoid mistakes—in advance. The listener opens his mind to idea input so that he can develop the best possible plan. A secretary, asked about a proposed new office form, shows how it can be adapted to her needs—and the company has a better form. A foreman describes a way to modify a stock handling system—and the company has a better system.

Unquestionably our open society and democratic form of government provide the logical rationale for this consultive aspect of listening. The American man in the street does not change fundamentally when he goes to work in an organization. He wants to be consulted on matters that concern him just as he is allowed to speak out in his society. He wants to have a voice in what is passing around him.

Fifth, listening has as a main goal that most simple of all targets—get the job done and get it done right the first time.

> The manager of an aluminum die-casting plant received an order from top headquarters. He was told to cut his foreman force by 15 percent. He called in his chief aides and "noodled" the question: How to implement the order most acceptably and equitably, with the least damage to morale, loss of productivity, or other adverse effect?
>
> The ideas came in. The plant manager developed a seven-point plan that covered every aspect of the cutback. He put it into effect, moving through the phases of announcement and explanation (the cutback was necessitated by business conditions), a private conference with every foreman who would have to be let go, redistribution of areas of control of those remaining, and so on. Shortly afterward, he received feedback from the remaining foremen and from the work force: the extraordinary efforts he had taken to respect the rights of individ-

uals and to provide for their futures insofar as was possible had made a tremendous impression throughout the plant. Just as importantly, productivity did not decline and morale did not sag; productivity even rose slightly.

In a sister plant making the same cutback, management failed to take the same listening precautions. Morale plunged. Productivity went down drastically, and stayed down for months.

In such cases the manager has no second chance.

Sixth and finally, listening answers the need for a "selling" technique that may mean success or failure on any given project.

President Truman spoke of "persuasion." Other examples from politics include the case cited by Nichols and Stevens in their book *Are You Listening?* In that instance presidential candidate Adlai Stevenson traveled the country, meeting with Democratic Party leaders and largely listening to them. Many of them came to these meetings opposed to Stevenson's candidacy, but most of these left the meetings convinced that Stevenson was "their man."

Look at a case from industry.

> Executive Allen had under consideration a whole new research and development program that would entail major changes of emphasis and, eventually, entry by this rubber products company into new product lines. Impetus for the "new look" was coming from Sales. But then, Executive Allen learned, the director of research got wind of the proposed change and took umbrage before he even knew what was involved.
>
> Executive Allen didn't wait. He called in the D.R. and sketched out what was being considered. "This seems to have excellent possibilities," Allen told the D.R. He laid out the good market reasons that seemed to point to the need for changed emphasis. He asked the D.R. to take a week or so to review the draft plan and make recommendations. He listened, letting the D.R. talk out his ire. When the draft plan came back a week later, it had undergone a metamorphosis; it called for much more sweeping adjustment of the research and development effort. *It had become the D.R.'s program.*

Other managers have used similar methods to obtain union collaboration, overcome opposition from their peers, turn employee indifference to interest and achieve many similar goals.

The "selling" factor enters into this listening function just as it enters into so many other areas of communication, of managing. But the listening manager recognizes what industry in general has begun to recognize over the past few years: employees, coworkers and bosses, cannot be "sold" as the television announcer tries to sell the unseen audience. The fast, one-way pitch will usually backfire. It will fail because it does not gain understanding and acceptance; it does not take into account the other's needs, thoughts, ideas. The waste in much communication stems exactly from this flaw. "There is massive evidence . . . that communication aimed at changing others (without the slightest possibility of even a small reverse influence) is effective only to a very slight degree," notes McGregor.[3]

In an Organizational Sense

Listening reaches its highest pitch of purpose as an instrument of organizational interaction. The manager listens specifically to build a more effective organization. For this reason the organizational purposes of listening number so many, and exhibit such diversity, that we can only hope to enumerate the most important. In the enumeration, necessarily, some repetition will occur; the organizational and the project goals cannot be wholly separated.

Different managers stress different facets of their own talents; they take different roads to the goals of personal and organizational success. For this reason it may help to examine your conscience again on the various purposes and goals that *you* establish for yourself. What long-, medium-, or short-range targets do you set for yourself and the organization? Into what context do they fall—whether operational, planning, sales, or

---

[3] Douglas McGregor, *The Professional Manager,* McGraw-Hill Book Company, New York, 1967, p. 153.

some other? Do they have a primarily people or human relations content—or some other? Good management does not appear under a microscope as one-celled and simple; on the contrary, it is problem, people, project, and profit. It is William Foote Whyte's "five M's"—men, money, machines, morale, and motivation. It speaks today with the voice of decision and tomorrow with the voice of inquiry. The day after it may speak with the voice of commendation.

Its major task remains, most simply, to direct and decide correctly in the light of the overall needs and realities of the organization and of the people in it. The manager who fires a subordinate has these goals in mind in discharging the man— or he brands himself as unprofessional. Same for the manager who launches a new product line, or who calls for expansion of operations.

Listening is the balancing pole that enables the manager to walk the tightwire to good decisions. With listening he can assess the needs of the organization against the needs of the individuals who make it up. Listening, like Theory Y, posits the belief that the needs and requirements of the organization can be fulfilled best where individual needs for self-fulfillment or self-actualization can themselves be best met.

> Many of management's best ideas are sown on cold and sour soil. Where attitudes and feelings are transmitted freely upward, however, management is forewarned of possible failure and can better prepare the seed bed before its own ideas are broadcast. Upward communication tells us not only when our people are ready to hear our story but also how well they accept our story when we do tell it. We have no better means than upward communication of knowing whether our downward communication has been understood, believed or accepted.[4]

The plant manager who toured his domain not long after giving a series of talks had these principles in mind. He also

---
[4] Earl G. Planty and William V. Machaver, "Stimulating Upward Communication," *Effective Communication on the Job,* American Management Association, New York, 1963, pp. 24–25.

had specific goals. Beyond all of them, he was consciously doing many other things as, with department managers, foremen on various levels, and production employees, he conducted his "pure listening" exercise. We can list these as the organizational goals any manager can set for himself:

- On the most practical basis the plant manager wanted information that he and his staff could use to make adjustments and changes, to plan and devise programs. He wanted, himself, to be informed.
- He was trying to release the creative drive latent, or already patent, in his staff. He believed, with many authorities, that creativity exists in all of us, but that it will be wasted if not actively sought *and used*.
- Through face-to-face contacts and communication he obtained his own personal reading of morale. He understood that morale has no uniform "level," but subsists in shapes whose dimensions differ from department to department, or work area to work area. As a matter of course he supplemented his personal findings with the data commonly provided in organizations, from records on waste, scrap and grievances to accident reports, training records, and so on.
- Employees, he believed, could entertain feelings of goodwill toward their company if given a voice, if heard. He tried deliberately but not unnaturally or obviously to encourage such feelings. From such feelings, he knew, sprang improved morale and all kinds of organizational benefits from higher productivity to improved quality.
- And beyond that he was trying to develop the involvement that leads to top performance. He wanted deep *interest* in, not shallow *attention* to, company goals. An individual's degree of involvement may vary greatly from month to month or day to day; but on an organization-wide basis the level of involvement can, within limits imposed by accident or incident, be increased and kept high by wise management.
- The plant manager was doing all he could to head off misunderstandings before they arose. The fullest possible exchange of information provided the means to that end, he believed. He believed he could minimize, if not totally prevent,

the misunderstandings and problems normal to organizational life.

■ The plant manager was aware that his responsibility for developing future managerial talents took priority over many of his other responsibilities. He sought to instill cool professionalism by acting the cool professional.

■ The plant manager was admittedly "company minded" in the sense that he wanted to see the plant and the company succeed and didn't care who knew it. He hoped others would make the same effort to superinduce company mindedness among their subordinates by *showing,* not *telling.*

■ Similarly, our plant manager wanted to see the "big picture"—but not to the exclusion of the "little things." The little things, he knew, made up the mosaic of the big picture. In the estimation of production workers and foremen little things could become major issues if not attended to. He wanted to train his subordinates to take a broad view without writing off what appeared to be minor elements and issues. This, to him, differentiated the boys from the men in managing, the mature from the immature, the perceptive from the unperceptive.

■ In all these ways he stressed preparedness for the future, self-training for the unknown and unexpected. The future hurtles on—at the manager; he did not want to stand in its way, or be unprepared for it. On the contrary he wished to welcome it. He stressed continual rethinking, continual reassessment, continual recharging of the communications batteries.

■ The plant manager saw a double advantage for the organization, psychologically, in encouraging full participation by all employees in the communication process. First, the employee enjoyed the "therapy" of free communication itself: what the Greeks called *catharsis.* And second, the employee, feeling better because he could communicate freely and without restraint, approached his job with greater enthusiasm. The two effects wound back on one another, with mutually reinforcing results.

■ "Thinking success," the manager believed, must precede

real success; he wanted his organization to think success. To that end he communicated—listened—in such a way as to encourage success-oriented attitudes. He had seen organizations where management and production staffs both had lost interest in their companies' futures because they were cut off from top management's essentially optimistic thinking. He wanted to avoid such a development.

- He was seeking to inculcate in his people a spirit of teamwork. He felt that achievement grows out of cooperation. Listening gave him a practical kind of cooperative communication which, properly used, could lead to tighter physical and moral cooperation and integration.

- The plant manager wanted, by example, to show others how to listen. He understood the truth of the comment, "We must never forget that the most powerful communication isn't what you *say*, it's what you *do*." [5]

- Most basically and finally, the manager believed in his secret heart that man is not a machine and that his humanity must be recognized. He tried to put the principle into practice. He fundamentally recognized his coworkers as *people* and dealt with them as individuals.

To build individual effort into smooth group effort. To provide the future leadership of the company. To provide for the future operationally by keeping planning and programming up to date in terms of knowledge of the organization and its capabilities. To do all these things continuingly and in such a way as to make repeated effort productive through greater competence in interpersonal communication. These sum up the organizational goals of listening.

In a Personal Development Sense

We have discussed the goals of listening in reference to specific projects and in reference to the organization as a whole. The art of listening has equally compelling reasons for existence from the point of view of the manager's own development. We

[5] Frank E. Fischer, "A New Look at Management Communications," *Personnel,* vol. 31, no. 6, May, 1955, p. 495.

can consider them under four main headings: Competence, Leadership through listening, Toward more complete understanding, and Integrity.

1. Competence The statistical proofs of the importance of listening have spillover in the area of managerial competence. As shown, communication occupies the major portion of the manager's or executive's working day. Listening, as the key phase of communicating, occupies from 45 to 63 percent of that communication time. It follows that listening does more than vaguely contribute to the manager's never-ending search for on-the-job competence.

Skill at listening may actually put the final seal of authenticity and sincerity on the manager's claim to—and absolute need for—increasing competence. Attention *must* be given to listening and its disciplines if the manager is to qualify as dedicated in the search for widening proficiency. "If managers only knew it, they could actually increase substantially—even double—their effectiveness if they would control their tongues and really listen," an executive told me once.

What we are suggesting is that one-way communication—communication without effective listening—is probably doomed to partial or substantial failure. It amounts to talking at, not talking with, another. Unless the manager possesses an inordinate fund of luck, to the point where his faulty communication methods cannot destroy or damage a halcyon situation, the risk of nonlistening is not worth the candle. The manager, like it or not, nourishes or stifles communication in his organization. To the extent that he nourishes it by example and precept, and policies and action, he will probably succeed as a manager. To the extent that he stifles it, he will probably fail as a manager.

But neither success nor failure comes about instantly. Each develops over months or years. Success does not snap to your command, nor does failure always follow inevitably and immediately on incompetence. We can even say that some incompetents will never be discovered; many "competents" will never be rewarded adequately. But we have to look at the typical or average case in which competence both exhibits itself in managerial success and is rewarded—somehow.

2. Leadership through listening   The three masks worn by managers as leadership styles—democratic, autocratic, and free-rein—are not mutually exclusive. They may all appear in one manager at different times. A democratic leader may have to give a flat order. An autocratic leader may consult with his subordinates occasionally on the best ways to reach a predetermined goal. A free-rein leader may "get tough" and fire a man for neglecting his duties.

Nonetheless, the styles of most managers fall into one or the other of the three basic patterns. A manager stamps himself as "autocratic," "democratic," or "free-rein" depending on how he *normally* and characteristically makes his decisions, on how he communicates generally, on how he leads. How he does all these things depends largely on how he listens. Ability to listen will probably give that individual style what effect it achieves over a period of time.

> Manager Joe is a true autocrat. A department manager in an aircraft manufacturing plant, he rants and raves and shouts at all his men equally. Orders pour from him like water from a fountain. He hates paper work. But his men respect him, and work as hard when he is attending a meeting "upstairs" as when he is tearing up the macadam in the department. They know that when they point out to him that a toilet has broken down, or a machine needs repair, or two workers are standing in a draft, he boots someone and has the problem rectified instantly. He also takes deep interest in his subordinates' private lives, and has been known to help in emergencies.

Is Joe really autocratic? He *leads* and his men follow because beneath his crusty exterior operates an inner, listening ear that tells him how to be fair and concerned and when to act for his men.

> Manager George speaks softly and never carries a big stick. As shop supervisor in a printing plant, he communicates with his people from the safe refuge of his office. He figures men are

men and as workers they "should act like men." He thinks in terms of charts, symbols, schedules. His men have little respect for him; nothing ever changes in the department, except that the equipment grows older, the walls become dingier, the presses and other machines slowly fall apart until they have to be taken out of service, and there's water on the floor where the roof leaks. George knows the men want improvements, but "They're men and they should be able to work without all this bitching."

Is George really a free-rein leader? Is he a leader at all? He never raises his voice, but he never listens either.

Manager Frank believes in consulting with his men on anything he knows is of importance to them. He does not spend much time at it; but he does it well. He keeps them informed personally or through the supervisors and aides who help him run his department in a large electrical machinery plant. He uses the bulletin boards and the plant newspaper when that is called for. Within the department he actively seeks the ideas of those with whom he works. All at once, orders to the department fall off drastically. Frank faces the difficult alternative of dropping the small night shift crew entirely, at least for a short period. He consults with his superiors, makes his decision, and informs the men concerned *in person* that in two days they will be laid off. The men basically accept the action and believe Frank's rationale for it.

Is Frank's democratic style of leadership vitiated, or even temporarily violated, by his drastic action?

To ask the real question: Don't the varying degrees to which the three managers listen—the varying degrees of skill and continuity—really determine how well their leadership "takes" and is accepted?

Listening in these three managerial equations cannot be disregarded. It must be held to be the most potent tool in the manager's chest of leadership aids. It can humanize the most abrasive style; its absence can nullify the possible good effects of the gentlest style. We come then to three closely related generalizations:

■ Listening, done well, enlarges the manager's leadership

capacity; it tells him when to act, show concern, adapt to circumstance—and how to do these things.

- In so doing it becomes what has been called a "projection of leadership"—the characteristic of a leadership style that is most intimately and frequently felt by others, the characteristic that enables the manager, whatever his style, successfully to mesh by adjustment with those around and under him.
- In the constantly shifting kaleidoscope of modern business and industry, listening performs the essential, if very personal, function of readying the conscientious manager for change. This listening manager, because he listens well, has his mental stethoscope on the heartbeat of the organization and can usually predict what changes are needed and will occur. He avoids the trap of being "shut off . . . from the most vital listening ability of all—the ability to observe, sense and apprehend change, the ability to hear the whisper of the future."[6]

3. Toward more complete understanding No matter with whom he is communicating, the manager seeks to do two things: to understand and to be understood. It is likely that he can do neither, except on the most abecedarian levels of order dispensing and reprimanding, unless he listens. His ears will be closed. He is not geared to the acquisition of knowledge or understanding of what the other fellow is thinking, or even of adequate factual background.

It should be obvious how understanding lags if the manager does not take the time and trouble to listen: intake fails. Thinking and planning become work in a vacuum, a consummation that might be tolerable in a laboratory, where things or phenomena occupy the spotlight, but which can only handicap the man with people responsibilities.

It is not so obvious how the manager, no matter how blessed with goodwill, can fail to *be understood* if he has not learned listening. It can best be explained this way: on the in-

---

[6] George de Mare, *Communicating for Leadership—A Guide for Executives,* copyright © 1968, The Ronald Press Company, New York, p. 230.

terpersonal, face-to-face plane this manager runs at least three of the major risks that *organizations* face in practicing unlistening.

■ In not listening the manager runs the risk that he will make decisions that do not solve, but only complicate, problems; or that he may talk over or past another's head; or that he will ask performance that the other cannot or will not deliver. I listened once as a manager delivered an impassioned plea for "more management-union cooperation" to a group of union leaders. At the end one of the union men said: "Mr. Brown, I don't know what you're driving at. Our first job is to work for those guys out there." This manager simply did not know the reality of what lay at the other end of the human arena in which he was speaking. He could not possibly *be understood,* and heeded, in such circumstances.

■ He may project his own faulty communications approach through people who only make the communications matter worse. For example, the manager who tolerates a subordinate "bull of the woods" must be prepared to be tarred himself with the bull of the woods brush to greater or less extent. He cannot make himself understood, in that context, as anything but a bull of the woods. The National Labor Relations Board wisely makes managements take responsibility for all their supervisors' actions and statements in union organizing campaigns.

■ He may become insulated or isolated, find good decisions harder to make, and end up by making few or none. His few decisions may be ill-advised. He may send sprats to catch whales; his decisions fall short of the target. Though he may still see himself as a manager and decision maker, he is not viewed as such by those around him. He cannot be understood because his isolation drives a wedge between the realities of what others see and his own perception of himself.

In brief, the nonlistening manager does not fill out understanding. He does not practice the one art that could tell him whether he is getting across. And "successful communication . . . depends to a great extent on the ability of the communicator to perceive how he is being understood or why he is being misunderstood."[7]

4. Integrity To this point our analysis of the goals of listening have appealed to the manager's self-interest. They have been designed to show how the manager can "get the job done" better, or how he can give a major boost to his personal qualifications. Integrity in management and communication puts the question in a slightly different pigeonhole: That of general character, self-respect, and the need for the "whole man" in today's business world.

Consider how far our knowledge of human nature and human relations in industry has progressed. Once, The Boss was King. Later, starting about the 1920s, we moved through an era of rather self-conscious collaboration. The worker, it seemed, was to be placated with cooperative gestures. But still, at that stage, there was little respect for the worker as a human being. That too changed as writers like Mayo, Likert, Roethlisberger, and others began to apply the findings of psychology and other social sciences to the theory of management.

McGregor's Theory Y as enunciated in his book *The Human Side of Enterprise* made a powerful and convincing case for maturity in management and the employment of modern, supportive approaches to people. This was by now no fad; it looked to the long future of American business and industry. It grew out of the past in which many errors had been made, and many false gods worshipped. Few today decry it as transitory.

The researchers and experts did their research and experimentation in business and industry; they were not talking down from an ivory tower. They brought the old, simplistic, authoritarian approach through "scientific management" and further until an art was born. A body of technical knowledge came into being for those who would use it.

[7] Norman F. Maier and others, *Communication in Management*, American Management Association, New York, 1955, p. 169.

That body of technical knowledge stands available to any manager willing to learn it. It includes the techniques of communication; it has the goals of enabling the manager to work better with people and of making it possible for them to realize their potential in working with him. It rests on the proposition that in this way the organization itself prospers best. The manager today can hardly call himself "whole," or the possessor of integrity in reference to his job and his people, if he does not make use of that legacy of knowledge.

Rounding Off the Communications Fabric

Listening has still another purpose: to supplement all the other forms and phases of communication within the organization. It should not stand alone any more than the plant newspaper should stand alone as management's sole means of communicating with employees.

What purposes does listening serve in its function as an adjunct and supplement to other forms of organizational communication? There are three main ones:

1. It produces the feedback necessary to accurate understanding of how messages communicated in other ways have been received.

2. It suggests areas in which communication through other means, either oral or written, should be expanded, intensified, reduced, revised, or restressed.

3. It provides the guidance needed for adjusting the specific content of other forms of communication to the realities of the organization's situation.

An anecdote will illustrate how each of the three purposes may be served in a single communication exercise.

> A manufacturer of components for television sets launched a quality drive. Not long after the drive began, the president of the firm asked his department managers to listen for reactions to the drive. He also listened himself. The word came up: "Our people are accepting the drive and its goals with some reservations."
>
> The drive continued in intensified form. Its basic message,

"Quality Power," began to appear in other forms—posters, articles in the plant paper, buttons—as the president sought to reach employees in other ways. He kept checking through listening—his own and that of others. He found soon that employees were dropping their reservations, but not with the alacrity that the president wanted. On the basis of his listening finding that employees felt that "there isn't enough in this drive for me," he adjusted the content of the message to stress that theme more heavily. Employees learned in plant newspaper articles and in other ways that quality meant success with customers, more orders, and in the long run job security and even expanded job opportunities.

The feedback data provided by listening have importance whether the other means of communication employed are formal or informal, oral or written. And recognition of the importance of feedback can be built into some messages, underlining the manager's awareness of the need for it. A remarkable case in point was mentioned by authors Robert Newcomb and Marg Sammons:

The president of Pitney-Bowes, in a letter to employees, announced that the company was planning on switching from a weekly to a bi-weekly system of paying employees. This would clearly necessitate budgetary adjustments on the part of employees. The letter ended:
"I'm sure each of you will give this matter your earnest consideration, balancing any change it may require in your personal planning against the good of the company of which you are a part. *If, after that, a majority of you feel that the change should not be made, we will not make it.*" [8]

In another case the superintendent of a chemical plant sent a letter to all his management people a few weeks before negotiations were to start on a new union contract. His letter read in part:

"You know we have worked for an improved climate in our plant for the past year and a half. Any success we have

---

[8] Robert Newcomb and Marg Sammons, *Employee Communications in Action,* Harper & Row, Publishers, Incorporated, New York, 1960, p. 23.

achieved is due partly to your work and cooperation. We hope you will continue your efforts in this area . . . we will be contacting you in the next few weeks to obtain your ideas on how we can best approach negotiations. Our purpose will be to protect the interests of all employees while keeping in mind the needs and competitive stance of our company."

Listening and the broad base of communications No piece of communication, be it remembered, has value if it does not achieve at least four purposes:
- It must be heard, or received.
- It must be understood.
- It must be accepted.
- It must be acted upon.

Can we ever be certain that the four steps have been fulfilled without verifying through feedback—through listening as the key interpersonal means of obtaining feedback? The manager who launches a department-wide safety campaign will not, without listening, know how the drive is taking effect in the minds of his subordinates; and it must take effect there to *have* real effect. At the lower level of a machine operation, it may be different. A foreman may be able to observe how a worker reacts to an order to "do all the PAL (Preferred Account List) orders first," and in that observation he may have all the feedback he needs. But even in this context listening could tell him how, to what degree, and why the machine operator accepts—or objects to—the order.

We must, in effect, add a fifth step to the four already enumerated if we want to make certain that communication is achieving its broad goals:
- It must be verified through listening.

No one disputes any more that communication must have clear-cut, well-defined aims. It seeks to move people, with all their human differences in personality, skill levels and aspiration, to outstanding achievement. Listening serves as a keystone in this goal-oriented structure. It seeks to set the listening manager or executive on top of his situation, in a position from which he can survey on the basis of knowledge, devise on the basis of reality, and communicate to take advantage of that reality. And here we have a final note on the why of listening: the manager pursues this arcane art for primarily positive, not negative, aims just as he operates along the whole broad base of communications for positive reasons.

The Hawthorne experiments of the 1920s and 1930s made history. Among other things, they showed that the individual's perceptions of the facts of his work situation—how he feels about them, what he finds objectionable in them, what he believes about them—are more important than those facts themselves. Listening provides the means of finding out how the individual perceives those facts.

This goes to the heart of our case for listening. The manager learns it to understand better the human material with which he is dealing. He learns listening for the same reason that he learns communication of any kind: to be able to manage people better.

3
The Listening Mind

> What the heart contains, the mouth uttereth.
> —Proverb

THE MANAGER IS THE UBIQUITOUS "THEY" to whom workers endlessly refer when they talk of upper management. Yet the manager differs little from the workers or the line supervisor in at least one respect: his mental perceptions of the facts of his role, his environment, and his own abilities rank as more important than the facts themselves.

"The manager's performance in his role is . . . a function of his assessment of his own capabilities. Again, of course, this is a matter of his perception, not of objective reality. He may overestimate or underestimate the degree of any or all of his capabilities. He also makes subject evaluation of the importance of certain capabilities for the performance of his managerial job. . . ." [1]

[1] Douglas McGregor, *The Professional Manager*, McGraw-Hill Book Company, New York, 1967, p. 52.

In pursuing expertness at listening the manager works consciously or unconsciously in a parallel fashion. "I can listen," he tells himself, and goes, very properly, at the business of listening. As with managing itself, however, he can progress more rapidly if he knows initially what characteristics of mind should be assessed and developed. At that point, with the optimization of his own and of his organization's effectiveness as the goal, he can ask himself the real questions:

"Have I those mental characteristics that make for good listening? Have I those characteristics to the degree that I can build on them?" The more closely his answers correspond to reality, the better the start he has made.

Learning which are the important characteristics becomes the manager's first task. In ticking off the ingredients of the listening mind he should understand that moderate development of the various characteristics may suffice to qualify him as a learning listener. From there he can build more stately mansions.

Remember, too, that everyone possesses each characteristic at least to a minimal degree. There is bad and good, wise and foolish, generous and miserly in each of us: something of both the best and the worst. Development of the best is the goal.

Honest self-assessment as preparation for listening should have sought to clarify for you whether you could in a general way believe in and work toward highly developed listening ability. With that preparation behind you, you can look at those characteristics of mind that require specific inventorying and development.

THE OPEN MIND

"To achieve good listening I stress to myself the importance of candor and the open mind," the personnel director of a medium-sized manufacturing firm told me once. He had identified the key characteristic of the listening mind: what we might call "acceptingness." The manager or executive must have an accepting mind because his basic function is to make good decisions on the basis of learned data. Much of these data come through listening.

Heavy emphasis has been placed on analysis of the decision-making function in recent years. This responsibility sets the manager apart. It does so because it forces the manager to move in areas where accuracy of judgment can mean the success or failure of the department, the division, the entire organization.

Not that others in the organization do not have decision-making roles; they do. It is simply that the manager, standing higher on the ladder, decides the major questions: in which direction, and how, and how fast, and with what facilities and personnel will the organization go?

The decision maker, however, must base his decisions on *something*. This something we call evidence, or information. Enter listening as the means of obtaining evidence in oral communication; enter acceptingness as the mental characteristic that permits evidence to pierce to the listener's stock of knowledge and become part of it. In this way information actually becomes part of experience; it guides decision making and assists in the task of making sense of the incoming data.

Knowledge and experience: we come upon a key point here. Normally we regard "experience" as synonymous with seniority, as the amount of time spent on the job or on other jobs of a similar nature. But comments and statements found in the literature on management philosophy and techniques suggest that knowledge equates also with a kind of experience: a pseudoexperience. The experienced department manager may be the one who most rapidly absorbs the cost, equipment, personnel, and other factors in his departmental picture; he may be the one who most rapidly broadens his store of knowledge of the unit. The experienced sales manager may be the one who most quickly grasps the essentials of the challenge facing him.

So the time element in experience dwindles in importance. The manager seeking to "achieve experience" may be the one who practices listening with consummate skill. He may be that one because he is able to range widely in a short time across all the available sources and absorb what they have to offer

No wonder an experienced executive advises a man who is entering on a new managerial job: "Listen first, talk later." No wonder the business world looks upon the highly educated college student as a prize to be pursued and won. These attitudes merely reflect the fact that knowledge correlates with a type of experience, however that knowledge was acquired in terms of time.

Ingredients of "Acceptingness"

What, then, are the ingredients of the open, accepting mind that seeks to absorb new evidence, new experience most rapidly? What must a manager do to develop an accepting mind? His efforts should move in five main directions:

- Development of the habit of transactional communication.

In transactional or genuine two-way communication the listener leaves open the possibility that he can change in response to what he hears. He remains amenable to change of mind, or idea, or approach when such change becomes justifiable. The input from others has equal or nearly equal weight to the ideas and attitudes he himself brings to the listening process.

- The practice of humility based on respect for others as people and as functioning parts of the organization.

Humility does not proceed from self-abasement but from recognition of one's own humanity; humility does not require love or tenderness, or anything more than acceptance of another's fundamental claim to humanity and individuality. In listening we give another's ideas and attitudes houseroom. It is doubtful that we can do this well unless we can view that other person as fundamentally equal to us, and deserving of respect, in the most basic way: as a person.

The case of one manager illustrates what happens when humility disappears and the would-be listener begins to look down on or stereotype another person. "I can't respect Joe as a person any more," this manager told me. "Not after what he's done." At that point the manager, an excellent communicator, found himself incapable of truly listening to Joe, a fellow member of management. He admitted it.

- Willingness to inspect every piece of evidence coolly to avoid rash or poorly conceived decisions and action.

The willingness to examine every piece of evidence or information—even conflicting material—that could be useful puts the listener on the pedestal reserved for the thorough and thoughtful worker in any line of work. Halfway measures can render a listening exercise ineffective just as they can lead to failure in any other area. The listening manager allows no preconceptions of his own to rule out an item of evidence. He neither scoffs at the boss's idea as "another brainstorm" nor rejects a worker's suggestion out of hand as "thought of before —no good."

- Cultivation of the ability to search out negative evidence —those attitudes, ideas, facts, and opinions that could prove the listener wrong.

This practice of the accepting mind seeks to rule out self-delusion; it circumvents the tendency among most of us to steamroller another's thoughts or opinions with ideas of our own. Hunting down negative evidence requires that the listener challenge his own beliefs and ideas by actively subjecting them to oppositional evidence. This type of effort ". . . is not easy, for behind its application must lie a generous spirit and real breadth of outlook," but in making the effort ". . . you are less in danger of missing what people have to say." [2]

- Deliberate pursuit of the mental and emotional equilibrium that takes the interior "static" out of listening.

Such static may or may not exhibit itself overtly. Always, however, it sets up resistance that interferes with your reception of another's words. The listener afflicted with lack of equilibrium or equanimity may "fly off the handle" and thus

---

[2] Ralph G. Nichols and Leonard A. Stevens, *Are You Listening?* McGraw-Hill Book Company, New York, 1957, p. 103.

most effectively shut off the process of communicating. By gesture or facial expression he may achieve the same unfortunate result. As a boss, you may impatiently terminate a discussion because someone has mentioned a word you dislike. Your static then may touch off static in the other; you may not be able to discuss a touchy subject with him at all—ever. Your loss of mental equilibrium, or "cool," has red-flagged his.

Ethics and the Accepting Mind

Ethical considerations may or may not enter into the question of accepting through listening. The listener who listens to augment his supply of evidence can perform as well as the listener who tries deliberately to *support* another through listening. You do not, in short, have to make Otto Pollak's thesis of "helpful other-directedness" your *primary* motive in listening. Pollak wrote:

"Instead of becoming other-directed in an exploitative way one might become other-directed in a helping way. For better or worse we have become perceptive of the psychological weaknesses of others. We perceive their anxieties. We are attuned to their depressive moods, to their ineptitudes in human relations, and we can spot their maladaptive defenses. To identify these weaknesses as challenges for our helping responses would seem to be an ethically appropriate reaction in our time." [3]

Ethically appropriate? Yes. Essential to success in listening? Possibly. Needed as the primary motive in listening? No.

We are arguing that the manager or executive can reasonably have pragmatic, selfish goals in mind in pursuing listening as a skill. He can seek self-development; he *must* have his own success on the job and self-aggrandizement as prime motivational factors. He *must* be working for the good of the organization.

He can do all these things, and should do them, without

[3] Otto Pollak, "The Protestant Ethic," *The Frontiers of Management Psychology*, Harper & Row, Publishers, Incorporated, New York, 1965, p. 35.

ruling out recognition of others' needs, others' rights, others' humanity. To paraphrase a statement of Clement D. Johnston of the United States Chamber of Commerce, we need not manifest our love for our fellowman while manifesting our concern for his welfare. The manager can manage, and listen in managing, without evangelizing. He can be supportive to others through listening for professional reasons more than for humanitarian—and not rule out the humanitarian. This is merely a question of priorities.

THE THREE GRACES

Three other qualities fuse in the mental makeup of the manager who listens effectively. The three are imagination, direction, and patience.

Imagination in Business and Industry

Much has been said and written on imagination or inspiration in the arts. Less has been written on imagination in business and industry. One could almost take away the impression that imagination has the ring of a dirty word when applied to the business/industrial milieu.

It just isn't so.

Everyone has seen or read of imagination in action on the magnate or superexecutive level. The biographies—the deeds—of some of the great tycoons have become part of both our American literature and of our national philosophy. The exploits of the Mellons and Carnegies, of the Rockefellers and Kennedys, have given rise to large bodies of both serious and satirical or critical literature. Horatio Alger still lives as a concept even if he has been made the butt of jokes.

True: the deeds that exhibit ruthlessness or lack of concern for others or overdedication to the pursuit of money have become the objects of critical evaluation as we have matured as a nation. But the energy and imagination that inspired the doers have nonetheless found imitators in every walk of our life. And rightly so.

That imaginative quality leads to healthy innovation, to creativity. It must exist at the managerial level if it is to exist in the organization at all. As we shall see, it provides the answer to the knotty problem of adapting to change. A big and often imaginative idea lies behind every major innovation or improvement that an organization attempts. Imagination also supplies the quintessential element in the innovational temper that Arthur Hyde of General Mills once called the lifeblood of any growth business. That temper must filter through all an organization's channels. It should produce ideas at every level of responsibility, from the lowest to the highest, from idea men in research and from workers who can be encouraged to rethink their jobs. Such rethinking occurs when a man takes a coldly critical look at everything he does, every move he makes, every tool and method he uses. As Hyde also notes, the objective is to find a better way.

How better to take a coldly critical look at accepted methods of doing things than by listening to others' views on how to do them? To listen to divergent views, to consider them, to accord them a place alongside the manager's own thoughts actually invites the imaginative solution. As Nichols-Stevens point out, the whole principle of brainstorming evolves from this truth. Participants in a brainstorming session must contribute imaginatively, insofar as they are able to. Whatever the real, long-term value of brainstorming, and it has been somewhat discredited, many managers and executives have been stimulated by it.

Why not let one idea lead into another? Why not let castles of ideas rise where wasteland stretched away into the idea-distance? As we shall see, the manager or executive in pursuit of imaginative decision making should at one stage of the creative process give his ingenuity free rein; he should cast about in the widest possible range of alternatives before settling on a course of action.

Thus the imaginative listener allows himself to be carried forward—not merely to mentally tape-record. He allows his own creativity to be triggered by what he takes from another. His mind, while receiving, is also searching for the better idea. He will later make his decision, and in many cases will even sketch out the proper method of implementing it. But in his listening he becomes the living answer to the universal business need described by Minute Maid Corporation's John M. Fox: "Business is looking for men who can think. There are many synonyms for this quality. It is sometimes called vision —also imagination. . . . To be a good manager, the ability to think creatively, constructively and clearly is essential. The leadership role in management calls constantly for resourcefulness." [4]

Direction: The Pursuit of Excellence

An anecdote illustrates the meaning of direction, the second of our three mental graces.

> A major publishing firm hired a young man who had no experience at selling but who knew he wanted to sell. Specifically, he wanted to sell the books the firm published. The young man had just come out of college, the Great Depression was on, and job applicants were plentiful. But the company took the young man on.
>
> He compiled an excellent record. He became a district sales manager, a regional sales manager, an officer of the company and finally, after twenty-five years, president and chairman of the board. "Now," he said at this point, "I'm at last able to start really influencing what goes into our books."
>
> Throughout his career this man had submitted ideas on the content of the books, a major reference set. Some of his ideas found acceptance, others didn't. But he never forgot that he wanted to pursue editorial excellence as well as professional excellence in sales. All through the years he had gathered ideas for editorial changes *by listening to the people to whom he sold the books*. He believed his listening skill, matching his sales expertise, helped him reach the top despite normal company vicissitudes.

[4] John M. Fox, "What It Takes to Be a Manager," *Vital Speeches of the Day,* City News Publishing Co., Southold, N. Y., Apr. 1, 1956. p. 376.

This executive exhibited the purest kind of direction. He contributed ideas steadily and gratuitously; he kept his eye on the main chance. He listened unfailingly—to equals, bosses, subordinates, customers. He worked to make his product the best on the market, and rejoiced in his ultimate accession to the company's highest active post primarily because at that point he could take more direct action to achieve that end.

Odiorne believes three factors go to make up such an executive's sense of direction:

1. *Strong goal orientation.* The person who will probably have the greatest success in overcoming obstacles has established some clear cut goals for himself, and is determined to achieve them. The fact that he's faced with the same red tape, difficulties and suggestions for delay that have stopped others doesn't faze him in the least. . . .

2. *A callousness to defeats.* The good obstacles hurdler normally has a built-in optimism that makes such things as inertia, opposition, confusion, timidity and ignorance mere details to be brushed aside or otherwise managed.

3. *Decisiveness.* The most pernicious trait a manager can have when faced with obstacles is indecisiveness. Very often this is explained away as a need for mature consideration of the situation, but actually indecision is the result of the mind slipping away into inappropriate or trivial matters. He may find that ordering a new desk or settling a squabble between two secretaries is much more intriguing than writing the order, or picking up the telephone to announce his decision. The obstacles hurdler makes his decisions when he can—and the sooner the better.[5]

As with managing itself, so with listening. The good listener should have strong goal orientation. He should be callous to defeats and decisive both in the development of a listening style and in acting on the information obtained. Strong goal orientation, in particular, implies the desire to build, to move forward, to learn and grow.

[5] George S. Odiorne, *How Managers Make Things Happen,* Prentice-Hall, Inc., Englewood Cliffs, N.J., 1961, p. 39.

Patience, The Sine Qua Non

Patience leavens determination and direction. Patience gives effort and goal orientation the quality of enduringness. Patience in listening is the *sine qua non* of success. It does not equate with simple optimism; rather, it serves as the mental characteristic that ensures that obstacles cannot become insurmountable nor failures destructive. It makes listening a long-term habit more than a one-shot or sporadic exercise.

Patience, finally, rules out the impatience that causes some managers to listen and work in manic spurts. The man who manages and listens this way typically has a weak hold on his subordinates. His inconsistency produces insecurity. When acting in "low gear," he may nullify the progress he may have recorded while in "high gear."

> The president of an industrial supply firm had built a going business in six years. To start out he had left a firm that, he believed, didn't reward him adequately. His own business expanded rapidly, but by fits and starts. In one period new customers turned up in droves; then for months nothing would happen. The president succeeded, however, in building an effective sales staff, and sales lay at the heart of the business. At a time when it was billing some $3 million a year, the company came to a major corner in its history: at an annual sales meeting the salesmen agreed vocally—even vociferously—that new product development should be stressed, and stressed hard, for the immediate future.
>
> The president disagreed. He had come far on the old products. He spoke his piece, refusing even to consider or listen further to the salesmen's proposals. The sales force had to accept the decision, and did. But within days the president went into a "low" mood in which his feeling of defeat and inertia called up bogeys and hobgoblins of conspiracy and revolt. Without warning, the president fired his national director of sales. Within months, seven of the nine top salesmen in the company had resigned. In a year the company was billing only $1 million and was struggling.
>
> The president never saw that his own lack of patience, the

impatience that made it impossible for him to listen when he was "high," with the resulting fear of simple disagreement, had wrecked the organization's growth potential.

Patience, in short, should enable the listening manager to ride out his own feelings of urgency, of short-temperedness, and of insecurity to do the job of listening—and managing—completely and properly. Unlike the president in our anecdote, the patient listener will not exhibit a fits and starts mental approach to his work.

Can training and self-discipline cure the kind of impatience that leads to rash and hasty judgment, inability to listen another person out, overemotional reactions, and so on? Few doubt it today. The plethora of courses in subjects ranging from Human Relations in Management to How to Use a Business Telephone and on to sensitivity training indicates deep faith in the power of education and self-development. Unmentioned as a condition precedent to the success of such training, however, is patient application: the self-discipline required in personal change or improvement of any kind. Desire precedes achievement.

The individual manager's potential for such self-discipline may depend on his degree of motivation, a function of attitude. Self-disciplined dedication can move mountains and teach volumes. This is nothing new. In the opinion of many authorities top management needs "complete objectivity and complete professionalism." But self-interest is not ruled out.

Greed, Not Altruism

Unless he is independently wealthy or extraordinarily unworldly, the individual manager must want to succeed as a manager/listener at least partly for reasons of self-interest. If he does not, he will probably fail. Even when he is developing the capacity of others to fulfill their own needs within an organization, he should have some personal motivation rooted in greed, or self-interest, or self-aggrandizement—call it what you will. It is asking too much to suggest that the executive or manager can divest himself of purely personal motives of gain.

"What makes a top executive run?" asks Feinberg. "It may be prestige, power, money. It may be a natural bent or yen for leadership. . . . It may be exercise of the divine right of kings or a man's need to prove he's escaped from under his father's shadow. Obviously, there is no one answer to the question. . . ."[6]

The three F's of "food, family and fame," then, can provide *some* of the drive that turns an executive's wheels: selfish goals tied to the concept of personal success through increased job or money recognition. Grant that; grant that pure altruism will almost never be found to be the main spark firing a man to consistently top-notch performance. This has to be true if only because business is founded on the profit motive and individuals normally share that motive.

There's still one best reward: success. The company's success and the individual's. For best results in listening, the desire to achieve both should be conjoined. One of the best managers I have ever seen in action sought personal financial success persistently. He listened to be able to move higher. He took from those around him what they had to offer—and gave credit where it was due. He had a record of creative problem solving. He followed a course of what has been called "enlightened self-interest" in his managing and listening: he wanted to do well personally and he wanted the organization to prosper. In listening he actively encouraged others to talk; he had found that under such circumstances the others gave continually more. He became a top executive in his firm. Because of his power of commitment to his own and his organization's success, he made the best kind of listening manager. And in listening he retained the common touch that made others *want* to contribute.

The listener, then, has some sense of personal and group mission. He conscientiously hunts and scratches for knowledge of others and of their thoughts so he can employ that knowledge for his own and the organization's good. In the typical

[6] Samuel Feinberg, *How Do You Manage?* Fairchild Publications, Inc., New York, 1965, p. 15.

case he mixes personal ambition with organization loyalty.

Are we downgrading the manager's contribution by admitting the pulling power of money? Not at all. We are only saying that money provides a bench mark by which the manager judges whether he is moving toward his goals. But he stays with an organization or leaves it, generally, on the basis of at least five touchstones of personal job satisfaction:

The work itself
Recognition
Achievement
Responsibility
Advancement

Now we are coming closer to the point where we can fit listening into the overall psychology of the manager. He can work for a better dollar. He should be engaged in the organization's work psychologically, at least to the extent that he wants to see it succeed as he succeeds. When the board of directors scrutinizes the Profit and Loss statement of his department or plant, sheer pride should impel him to want to know that the board members smile.

In the much-bandied phrase, he should want job satisfaction, that sense of accomplishment, growth, and development that comes with a good discharge of challenging job responsibilities in an atmosphere of openness and approval. This climate or atmosphere cannot be overstressed. The manager or executive assessing his mental or psychological adaptability to listening should note that in learning listening he will be gaining in the capacity to contribute to and produce such a climate. He may stand or fall, live or die, on his success in doing so. The climate he produces for his subordinates will probably determine whether the good men stay or leave. "One of the fundamental characteristics of an appropriate managerial strategy is that of creating conditions (climate) which enable the individual to achieve his own goals . . . *best* by directing his efforts toward organizational goals." So speaks McGregor.[7]

---

[7] McGregor, *op. cit.*, p. 78.

The Courage to Listen

The penultimate characteristic of the thinking of the psychologically attuned manager requires illumination of a key point: genuine listening asks for criticism, either direct or indirect. The listener says, by word or tone, gesture or act, that he wants free and open communication *whether what is said agrees with his views or not.* He declares himself ready to receive what comes his way; his temper may have to be leashed and his tongue may require continuous admonition.

> The steel industry has long been known for its action-oriented managers and foremen. At every level men seem to have been fed intravenously with the metal they are pouring, hammering or casting. In consequence hard-line management has become traditional.
>
> Bill, superintendent of a plate mill, broke the mold. He had come up through the ranks, but had more education than many of his peers. In meetings with his foremen he established a permissive atmosphere in which everyone not only could, but *was expected to,* say his piece. Top management would have cringed to hear what went on.
>
> "Bill," a turn foreman would say, "this inspection system stinks. We're letting stuff go through that I wouldn't ship to a junkyard."
>
> "I set it up," Bill replies. "Let's improve it. Ideas?"
>
> The group chimes in. Some of them yell to make themselves heard. They know no other way to talk. Bill makes a note now and then. When the din dies away, he points his pencil at a man sitting in the corner. "What do you think, Tom?"
>
> Tom speaks. Almost as soon as he starts to talk, one of the other men groans: "Come on, Tom, stop giving us this dream stuff."
>
> Bill speaks quietly to the man who addressed Tom. "We heard from you. Now we're going to hear this man out."
>
> Soon after, the meeting ends. Several men have assignments: check this out, make sure that gets done. The men go out laughing. One man says, "I always feel better after one of Bill's meetings. He really lets you blow your mind. You can knock him down and stomp on him and he never gets his feathers up unless you bust up his way of working."

Unless you bust up his way of working. Nothing else "got Bill's feathers up." He had the courage to face whatever came his way, and it was plenty in that department. But he stood up for the listening method that he had developed into a high art. Unless it was violated, he never succumbed to the pressures boiling around him. He had the courage to hear his own ideas challenged.

This man too went far in his company. Men who worked for him tried to follow him so they could continue to work for him.

Bill saw listening as a normal method of encouraging men to participate, in passion or anger if they had to, in the work of the plate mill and the company as a whole. He saw listening as the road to personal growth. He had the maturity that enables a manager to set an entirely alien pattern of management in an authority-ridden environment.

He also listened because he wanted to test his own self-control, without which he knew he could not control or influence others. He drew the self-confidence that he could exercise total control from repeated experience. Like the track star who dedicatedly ran ten miles every day, he sought the occasions for practice. Where many of his colleagues covered their inability to listen, or their lack of other managerial qualifications, with shout and bluster and threat, he faced what came his way. On the basis of his story we can now isolate the courage factors that go into the listening manager's mental makeup:

- He defies—accepts—the implied or direct threat in criticism, opposition, and conflicting idea.
- He tries in every possible way to grow and to mature so that at each step of the way he can sit atop the human sea of ideas, desires, passions, and ambitions that swell and simmer in his area of control.
- He self-confidently seeks to *test* his control of himself and others, through listening and in other ways.
- He faces the possibility that he may be wrong and remains prepared at all times to assess his own works, his own ideas, plans, and programs, as he would test those of others.

The fourth factor requires some illumination. The manager

who cannot change, or who will not, is in effect entering the listening exercise dishonestly. Most often he wants to convince someone else: to "sell" another person. To force his beliefs on his listenees. His communication has small chance of achieving its intended effect; it is "not transactional but coercive," as McGregor notes. No process of mutual influence takes place.

The courageous listener must be prepared to listen and weigh dispassionately and *take action* where feasible and advisable, even if in so doing he is wrenching his own thinking to conform to what he sees as a better way, a better idea.

With courage goes faith Dr. Arthur M. Cohen spotlights the final psychological qualification to be met by the manager-listener.

> If we think people are lazy, need controls, are going to try to 'goof off'—need to be directed all the time—we are going to behave in such a way that these things do happen, which in turn is going to lead people to behave in lazy fashion, to require many directives, and so forth. This confirms our original notion: they needed this direction. This is the self-fulfilling prophecy. . . .
>
> If we have a certain set of expectations about how people are going to behave or what motivates people, we act in such a way, even when not aware of it, as to produce behaviors on the part of those people which confirm our original expectations. . . .[8]

An immense weight of modern opinion backs up this estimate—and its corollary: that the manager who cannot convince himself in good faith that his comembers of the organization have the basic desire to perform well is going to have difficulty in listening. He will fall back almost inevitably on the "management by directive" approach that relies heavily on close direction from above. The "management by objective" technique, in which subordinates receive tasks and have the freedom to find their own best way to accomplish them, will

---

[8] Arthur M. Cohen, "Participative Management," *The Atlanta Economic Review,* February, 1968, p. 17.

be largely ignored. The directive-oriented manager's communications style will lean heavily on the downward phases, speaking and writing. But, worse, the portion of the organization that he influences will most likely assume the color and cast of his own approach. "Every organization is colored by the man at the top to a degree that very few of us would like to admit," comments Douglas Lynch of Brush Electronics.

Ask yourself the pertinent questions. Do you feel that every step in an operation must be spelled out? Do you feel the men around you and under your direct or indirect control must be watched all the time? Do you feel that they are trying to "get something for nothing"? Do you have a tendency to overspecify when you pass down an order?

Or can you manage by objective? Can you give someone a job and leave, within logical and expectable limits, to his better judgment the question of *how* it will be done? Can you give your right-hand bower, whom you know to be a specialist in sales promotion, the job of creating a new promo? How about the janitor? Does *he* need moment-by-moment direction? Or can you deal with him as a chemical company executive suggests:

"You can tell the janitor he has to sweep a floor every half hour, include the corners, run his broom over it a certain number of times (A alternative); or you can tell the janitor to keep the floor clean and use his best ways of doing it and get him to see the relevance of keeping it clean for production (B alternative)." [9]

If you can learn to manage by objective, accepting the basically sound motivation of the other man, you've qualified in one of the most difficult and basic tests of receptivity to listening. If not, if you *must* manage by directive, you may lack faith in the capacity of the other person to contribute validly. Listening may come hard. "To use this key (communication) we must have the faith that induced Charles McCormick to launch his plan of multiple management. We must act on the belief, as he did, that people can do anything if (1) they want

[9] *Ibid.*

to do it, (2) they are trained to do it, and (3) they understand the reason for doing it." [10]

Whence springs a manager's lack of faith in others? Most often from within, from the manager's own lack of faith in himself. This nontrusting, overdirective manager projects his own lack of self-trust into his environment. His actions hold a mirror to his mind.

This distrusting manager often projects very specific phenomena into his organizational environment. They add up to "demotivators" such as bureaucratic methods, rigid, narrow job definitions and a general unwillingness to experiment. These phenomena occur in organizations, but they begin with individuals; they start with *someone*. They may then become endemic to the organization, or to one compartment of it. The self-fulfilling prophecy of the nontrusting, overdirective manager may be turned into the sour reality of a "demotivated" work force or management unit.

Translating thought—and attitude—into action We are saying that your psychology has a direct effect on those around you and on the way in which they function. Unless you as the manager establish the conditions or climate in which "authentic" communication produces positive motivation for others, you may never see that motivation in your organization. "Authentic" in this usage means open, free, honest communication without fear that reprisal will follow or that advantage will be taken of the person communicating. Unless you as the manager can develop the faith in people that permits you to listen to them, to trust them, to give them their heads, to depend on their fundamental good will and will to work, you may find the task of establishing that "motivational" climate insuperable.

It must proceed from faith. Faith in yourself first; faith, secondarily, in the ability and willingness *and need* of others to do a job, to help the organization overall, and to help you as the boss by doing the work you want done.

---

[10] Frank E. Fischer, "A New Look at Management Communication," *Personnel*, May, 1955, p. 495.

A case history shows what can be done: how the reality of a managerial attitude of distrust can become the reality of a climate of trust.

> In a multiplant company based in New York State, one plant always seemed to be a problem child. For more than twenty years management and worker had, in Winston Churchill's phrase, "bayed at one another across a chasm." The plant employed more than 1,000 workers. It had a long record of strikes and labor unrest. It had a poor profit and loss record.
>
> A young plant manager joined the team. Convinced that the source of the problem lay with management, he convinced his director of manufacturing and others high up in the organization that the problem lay with management itself. He obtained permission to try what he called a "people approach." He put it into effect with little fanfare, but he personally carried the ball in announcing the new policy to supervisors; he saw them as vital cogs in the program he had in mind. What he told them, mainly: listen to your people. As the policy took hold, communications between union and management loosened; downward communications to workers became free, open, forthright. When the union's leaders came to the plant manager to suggest an all-plant picnic, the plant manager stopped them, smiling: "Let's do it," he said. Union and management joined forces in the Picnic Committee. Union-management cooperation became reality in other ways.
>
> Within six months the atmosphere of the plant began to change. One key department set a production record. Management continued to talk honestly and openly to workers. Within eighteen months the improved climate had spread throughout the plant. Through it all the plant manager geared all his communications, all his actions, to the thesis that most of his employees actually wanted to do a good job—really wanted the company to succeed.

One conclusion emerges not from this case only, but from hundreds of similar ones: managerial policies, management's strategies based on what it believes or refuses to believe, can hinder or facilitate self-actualization. Employees of any stripe work, or fail to work, in response to what they read as management's beliefs, whence spring management's policies and actions.

People orientation of the kind that succeeded in this true case proceeds from belief. This people orientation and its root belief also distinguish the listening mind.

People orientation comes hard or easily, depending on the individual manager. But most of us have it naturally, at least in some degree. Many managers have taken training in human relations; some have taken what has been called "sensitivity training." Such training is absorbed at least partly, even largely. It serves as the launch pad for expertise in listening, the communications aspect of a healthy people orientation. Beyond training, of course, most of us grow up with some people belief, some people orientation. To do otherwise would be all but impossible unless we grew up in separate jungles.

The task is to dredge it up, burnish it, put it on display, use it. In a practical sense, the task is to train oneself to more active employment of those mental attributes that make for good listening. In this way the healthy attitude and practice of the people-oriented, listening management can be translated into the supportive, action-based atmosphere of the really successful organization.

The critical faculty Needless to say, the listening manager does not throw away his critical common sense when he listens. On the contrary, he keeps it in high gear at all times. He may sharpen it through study. For example, many managers test what they hear against the guidelines laid down by the Institute for Propaganda Analysis. The Institute has identified seven different persuasive techniques that, unless recognized, could dull or render ineffective the critical faculty. The seven may be identified briefly:

1. *Name calling.* "If my opponent believes that, he must be a Communist."

2. *Glittering generality.* A conclusion that obviously has not been supported through rational, logical argument. "Every American supports the President's foreign policy."

3. *Transfer.* A speaker stands in front of an American flag,

suggesting by the process of transfer that he is a true patriot.

4. *Testimonial.* "Real he-men like John smoke our cigarettes."

5. *Plain folk.* A political speaker kisses babies, shakes hundreds of hands, and joins enthusiastically in the town festival, suggesting that he differs in no way from the rest of us.

6. *Card stacking.* The same political speaker may present only one side of an issue, or so much of one side that the other side appears idiotic.

7. *Band wagon.* "Everyone's going to vote for Jones. Don't be on the losing side."

How critical judgment comes into play will be discussed in greater detail in a later chapter. To be remembered now: The listening manager does not challenge every single word or syllable he hears. "Such mental activity would ruin comprehension, which lies at the very foundation of all listening." [11] The listening manager *does* foster and actively try to develop those mental characteristics that make listening not merely personally rewarding but productive organizationally.

[11] Nichols and Stevens, *op. cit.*, p. 138.

4
Creativity — the Element of Adventure

> The traveler has to knock at every alien door to come to his own, and one has to wander through all the outer worlds to reach the innermost shrine at the end.
> —Rabindranath Tagore

THE STORY HAS BEEN TOLD of the executive who felt he needed a raise. He went to his boss and made his plea. Concluding, he said: "There's one other thing. I'm always working like the devil and Jones just sits in his office, staring out the window and thinking."

"Listen," the boss said, "if you could come up with the ideas that Jones comes up with, you could just sit in your office and stare out the window and think too."

Jones, in other words, *created*. Can we add this element to the simple, unqualified listening we have been discussing? Can we add creativity as a subgoal of listening?

We can. We must and should. This is our thesis: that we

can develop an extradimensioned communication ability that enables the manager to step beyond the traditional, the platitudinous, and the ritualistic. The manager listening creatively does this; and he knows too that encouragement of creativity and its action counterpart, innovation, from any sources expands organizational potential. New ideas become building blocks. This manager works on the idea that development of the imaginative faculty that all men possess, in greater or less degree, helps by leading to new solutions to old problems.

How is creativity achieved in listening? By knowing the creative process. By using that knowledge to inform the manager's listening with awareness, first, of the possibility and need for creative answers and, second, of how to go about achieving them. By applying that knowledge so that the listening manager can see when he has achieved creativity.

Creative listening, in brief, differentiates itself from simple listening in the important sense that it adds creativity, the achievement of something new, something better, as a goal.

This extradimensioned listening relates closely to artistically creative effort, and we shall consider it as such. Listening, like artistic creativity, involves the effort to move beyond the existing or established; it takes what is already available and attempts to reorganize it—and adds elements that are actually new to it. Listening seeks to step out of or beyond the old order and scale new heights.

Creative listening, the "movement beyond the established" organizational ways of making decisions and effecting innovation, takes the manager into a land of adventure where the known and expected may assume new shapes. He takes the risks of creative decision making. When successful, he experiences an exhilaration comparable to that of the artist who discovers a new synthesis, a brilliant departure.

Such is the listening we shall be discussing from now on: creativity-oriented listening. Listening that not only dredges up the thoughts and opinions of others but also treats those thoughts and opinions as the raw material of inventive managerial decision making. Since the listening manager relates to the artist in a special way, is like him, and can learn from what the artist undergoes, we shall first examine artistic creativity.

ARTISTIC CREATIVITY

The concept of creativity in the arts has been deeply explored and heavily documented. Artists themselves have described the separate steps in the creative process. This process is usually seen as consisting of four basic phases:

1. *Preparation:* the research, search, and learning stage; the buildup or preliminary period in which the subject works for idea or inspiration.
2. *Incubation:* the period in which the spark of an idea starts to become visible; the gestative process.
3. *Illumination:* the phase at which the idea springs to life either partially or fully blown; the moment of insight.
4. *Verification:* the stage at which the artist seeks to translate the idea into concrete or sensible form; the phase in which the idea comes to life.

Authorities and artists themselves agree that the artist need not pass consciously from one stage or phase to the next. He may create almost unconsciously. Kipling told of a demon that took hold of his pen when his writing was going well. Painters have reported similar experiences. But generally artistic creation has had distinguishing characteristics.

For one thing, artistic creation normally has emerged as the by-product of consistently pursued inspiration. The successful artist who woos his muse occasionally and in dilettante fashion is the exception; more normally, this successful artist makes creativity the object of a continuing and intense pursuit. The moment of insight itself may come when least expected; but this does not mean it does not come as a consequence of unremitting prior effort. "If people knew how hard I have to work to gain my mastery, it wouldn't seem wonderful at all," complained Michelangelo.

For another thing, artistic creation has been found to be dynamic, not static. It functions even when it appears to be lying dormant. The creative process may go on beneath the silent surface just as water continues to flow beneath river ice. Artist after artist has told how he experienced inspiration on a bus, while at play, or while trying to get to sleep at night. Relaxation or play may undam an insight. This is what has been called the solving or resolving action of the sub- or nonconscious mind: the "transliminal mind's flash of illumination."

Finally, even though the stages of artistic creativity have been identified, we cannot always assume that they occur in a particular sequence. One stage may precede or follow another. The stages may be broken into parts, with some illumination, for example, taking place now and more taking place later. The stages do, nonetheless, serve as convenient starting points for the study of managerial creativity.

THE MATRIX CHANGES—SLIGHTLY

How does all this apply to creative listening as the road to creative management? Creative listening is to the manager what a basic technique is to the artist. Or as the backstroke is to the champion tennis player. Once he masters technique, the artist can go beyond it and build on it. But in managerial creativity employing listening as a key tool, we must add a step.

> In the winter of 1966–1967 and the spring of 1967, many companies across the country felt the effects of an "orders" recession in which inventories were drastically cut back. The manager of an electronics plant in the Midwest felt the orders cutback with dramatic suddenness. Suddenly, he was faced with the need to reduce his payroll by more than 20 percent.
>
> This manager, Andrews, had a special problem: he got along well enough with the union that represented his 600 workers, but the union was hard-nosed and tradition bound. It would, the manager knew, want management to proceed along well-established lines—to cut back according to the rigid seniority provisions of the contract.
>
> Andrews had other ideas. After three years on the job he had a deep regard for his workers—as people. From listening to

them, he knew they basically liked the company and his style of managing. But he had also learned that many of the good young workers feared a layoff. They had family responsibilities and needed the weekly paycheck; they would find other jobs. Many would be lost to the company.

From formulation of the problem Andrews proceeded through listening consultation with his department managers to a creative solution that involved four main steps:

1. He asked the union to approve a cutback that would entail shortening of the workweek for all workers instead of full layoff for a percentage of the workers. The union gave its approval after hearing the rest of the plan.

2. Andrews suggested that the union conduct a secret vote among all its members to obtain their consensus on the shortened workweek plan. The union agreed to conduct the vote on the theory that the workers would be making the decision.

3. In a series of plant talks Andrews personally explained to all his workers the alternatives—layoff by seniority or cutback in hours worked per week. Thus he made sure they would understand what was at issue. Andrew also personally guaranteed that the seniority provisions of the contract would not be affected in any way.

4. When the union vote came in, approving the shorter workweek by a narrow majority, Andrews posted the results on the bulletin boards. For the first time in its history the plant went on a four-day week. Not a single worker was laid off.

Andrews subsequently conducted a listening exercise at grass-roots level to ascertain the reactions of workers to the cutback. He found that even those standing high on the seniority roster —those who would not have been laid off anyway—both approved the method by which the cutback had been accomplished and enjoyed their three-day weekends.

Andrews's listening had given him the sense of the plant situation that he needed to understand that he had a problem in the first place. From there, listening to his managers and others, Andrews proceeded through the stages of plan development that an artist would have gone through to produce a work of art:

1. *Preparation:* Andrews restudied the contract and other fac-

tors in his situation to see if a solution might be found to the problem: how to save younger workers for the company.

2. *Incubation:* Andrews considered the problem—mulled it—and looked at possible alternatives. He did this with his top assistants.

3. *Illumination:* Even though time was short and a decision had to be made, Andrews slept on it for a couple of days. The plan, down to the detail of speeches that would let everyone know exactly what was at stake, came to Andrews one evening while he was reading a newspaper.

4. *Verification:* Andrews called in the union's leaders and presented the plan. He carried it out step by step from that point.

Was that all? Not quite. Andrews added the other step indispensable to good business creativity built on effective listening: he tested the water of opinion in the work force by listening personally and through his management staff. Here he changed the matrix as it must be changed in business creativity if results are to be measured and creativity is to be instructive for the future. Aligning the steps in artistic creativity alongside those normal to Andrews's type of business creation, we have:

Steps in Artistic Creativity	*Steps in Business Creativity*
1. Preparation—learning, research	1. Preparation—learning, research through the receptive communication skills of reading and listening
2. Incubation—the gestative process	2. Incubation—consideration of alternative plans, programs, projects in reference to a given problem
3. Illumination—the idea	3. Judgment formation—the idea or decision
4. Verification—realization of the idea	4. Order and follow-through—putting the decision into effect
	5. Evaluation—the assessment of results, reactions

The Added Element in Business Creativity

Andrew's *post facto* assessment represented the element that completes the creative cycle for the manager. But note:

Throughout the first two steps in both artistic and business creativity, the process of mentally testing, enlarging, twisting, adapting, rearranging, and substituting continues without pause. Possible solutions appear and are cataloged. In both types of creativity step 3, Illumination or Judgment Formation, identifies itself when the unessential drops away. A choice is made; you know what you want. "You have let your imagination soar and now you engineer it back to earth." The businessman decides that a new sales program will fill his need. Or that even this departure requires some innovations. Andrews hits upon the way to keep younger workers. As the president of a conglomerate once told me, "We looked at our resources for a long time. We talked over the problem of how best to utilize them, to make them grow. We decided then that we had to diversify to realize the potential in our very substantial base." For this man that decision became the moment of illumination.

In the fourth phase the artist captures his idea in the appropriate medium. He *communicates* his illumination, gives it form and substance. The manager does the same, but what he communicates is a plan, a program, an order, a solution to a problem. His action furnishes the answer to an organizational need, or difficulty, or challenge; it brings about a new organizational effort, a new policy, a production drive, a sales campaign, a staff restructuring. It may bring about many other things.

When the manager assesses the results of his decision and ensuing order in step 5, he is not only testing results. He is admitting that learning goes on all the time, even during the act of managing. He often sets aside time for the evaluation phase, scheduling a meeting or personally placing his finger on the pulse of the organization. He absorbs new information and may make the past decision the first preparatory or incubative stage of a new cycle of creativity. He *listens* to gauge the spirit, sense, and concrete effects of his decision. Unable to let well enough alone, or to assume that he has hit the mark, he does not let the appearance of success deceive or becalm him. He uses listening all through the creative process as a dowsing rod, as the sensor and source of continual input.

Creativity demands hard work. It cannot exist except in an atmosphere that outlaws inertia, makes an enemy of blind devotion to the tried, true, and conventional, and overcomes the fear of being different. Once the creative process is understood, drive or push—call it what you will—has more to do with creative success than either knowledge or great talent, authorities tell us.

Listening and sensitivity Both before and during the creative process the artist's work consists in *taking in* what he will later release as art. He learns technique and practices it endlessly. He mentally ingests impression, information, suggestion. His success as an artist then depends on three main things:

- His ability to absorb through his senses all that he will need when he comes to the act of creation: his sensitivity
- His ability to communicate within himself, to digest what he has absorbed and then to give it form in such a way as to evolve something new, artistically effective and true
- His mastery of technique in his chosen artistic specialty

The manager has a similar triad of requirements for success. But he functions in the workaday arena of business, commerce, or industry. He must, therefore, specialize in the task of absorbing whatever pertains importantly to the type of problem he will face. Within his business environment, like the artist in the artistic environment, he must, to be successful—

- Practice the receptive or assimilative communication skills of reading and listening to learn as much as is possible of the facts and realities he will be dealing with when he comes to create a decision
- Communicate within himself, or think, and practice the

expressive communication skills of speaking and writing to and with others, so as to communicate his thoughts and eventual decisions

- Know the art of managing

Listening in this context equates with the good artist's extraordinary sense perceptivity. It serves the same intake function.

Listening—road to originality Business annals teem with examples of original decision making based on creative listening. Company after company has tried something new because someone listened, saw a need, investigated, and created an effective answer to the need.

> A company in the northeast manufactured fabrics used for linings in certain leather and textile products. Long ago it recognized the possibility that its products might become obsolete. Rather than go the way of the buggy whip manufacturer, top management looked at the problem of what to do.
>
> The president of the firm consulted salesmen, his own executives, others. The competition, it became evident, would probably come from the plastics field. His eventual decision, evolved after months of listening, investigating, pondering: "If you can't beat 'em, join 'em." He founded a small subsidiary to manufacture plastic products of the type that could form his competition. Today both the parent and the subsidiary are in business, but the subsidiary has done better than the parent. Its annual sales total more than $20 million annually.

Another case shows how listening came into play to guarantee creative *communication* in one company. The case, cited by Newcomb-Sammons, concerns P. J. Paragon, president of Paragon Products Corporation.

During a thorough review of PPC's employee benefits program a question came up. "Mr. Paragon called in the personnel director and the treasurer" of the firm. " 'Now that our program is ready to roll, how do we go about this communication job?' he asked." After different possibilities were suggested, it was decided that management would put the same question to a benefit advisory committee of people from different parts of the organization.

The committee began to meet. "Through the committee," management "sincerely sought, considered and applied the ideas of their people," note the authors. "It did not take long to determine that they did not have plans simply for the sake of plans. . . . On the contrary, they had benefit plans designed to meet human needs, to help cope with some of the economic hazards—old age, illness or injury, death, and unemployment." The conclusion: ". . . We'd better be sure people can understand *why* they're getting these things, as well as *what* they're getting." [1]

A small thing? Not necessarily. It may have ensured that the company's large expenditures on employee benefits were not wasted.

A real estate man who understood creative listening told me of a case in which a few remarks by a client led to a major decision and—eventually—foundation of a multimillion dollar business.

"We were in a solid, growing local real estate business," this man told me. "But we were looking for ways in which we could expand significantly—into an entirely new area of real estate if possible. We had located land sites and done all the brokerage chores for four new motels for a major American hotel/motel chain when we got the clue we needed.

"At a ground-breaking the president of the chain mentioned to me that he wished he could find someone who could find motel sites in major cities overseas. He added that he didn't envy the man taking on the job, but that it could, over a period of time, prove lucrative. We questioned, listened, and offered to take on the job; we were "hired" as consultants and two years later founded a separate company to take care of all the international real estate business we had unearthed. By that time we were working for several dozen clients who

---

[1] Robert Newcomb and Marg Sammons, *Employee Communications in Action,* Harper & Row, Publishers, Incorporated, New York, 1961, pp. 110–111.

needed overseas real estate sites. That new business grew into a major enterprise in those two years."

Many authorities, of course, have noted that a creative idea lies behind nearly every major breakthrough or innovation in business, commerce, and industry. How could it be otherwise? Behind the reality stands the creative dream. Many of them resulted from creative listening.

Other differences are obvious Artistic creativity springs at least in part from the artist's *need* to create. This internal drive has expressed itself in many ways. Marcel Proust locked himself in a cork-lined room so that he would be free of drafts while pursuing the Muse of Writing. Toulouse-Lautrec lived the bohemian life of the people he wanted to paint. Many an artist has taken dope to learn what the addict experiences, and to be able to portray it accurately.

The manager finds himself in similar case—but without the same freedom to court experience. He cannot, normally, doff his business suit and white collar and work in the plant for a period of weeks, months, or years, performing his managerial job in the evening. Unlike Whiting Williams, the executive who quit his job to go to work as a laborer more than a generation ago, Mr. Average Boss today cannot surrender his post and prerogatives and start at the bottom. Job competition is simply too keen; he has too much invested in managership; and from a practical point of view the knowledge to be gained from such an experience, while valuable, might not be worth the loss of time and experience in management itself.

Creative listening bridges the gap between the deep involvement of the artist and the essential, needed involvement of the manager. In listening the manager can live, experience, sense the thinking and emotions of another person, or of a group. He must attempt to do this, in fact. He must "live into"—empathize with—the other's or others' problems, fears, and ambitions. Once he has learned this art, he becomes capable of seeing problems with another's eyes. He stands in the other's frame of reference.

The manager must make this effort at empathy because he

wants to make better business decisions, to move others to act. He is not writing a poem or carving a statue. He is part catalyst—Maxwell's demon, the agent of change—part teacher, part technician, part many other things. But as an important part of an organization, he has to interact with other parts of it—other persons in it—in such a way as to get results. He must further the organization's continuity. He has to build effective relationships.

This manager may have to make great decisions or small. In rare instances he will not be able to evaluate those decisions for years—perhaps not even in his lifetime. A captain of industry, for example, may decide that his company should take an entirely new direction in research and development—and do so in the knowledge that results cannot be obtained in any great measure for many years.

Great decisions or small, if the decision depends on deep knowledge of others, and if the manager has made them in the creative listening context that seeks such knowledge through empathy, through "feeling with" others, he can know he has considered the total human equation along with the other technical, social, methodological, and other considerations that must be counted and accounted for.

Avoiding traps There is a negative side to this coin. Managers who listen creatively avoid many of the traps inherent in organizational life. They may, for example, avoid the trap of assigning a task to an individual who carries a title but who cannot do a specific job, or cannot do it passably. A foreman may be exactly the wrong person to pass on to workers data concerning a change in company policy. The creatively listening manager may also avoid the trap of overloading—and even destroying—a colleague or subordinate. "Bringing people along" requires a deft, sensitive touch.

Listening managers may also avoid the trap of too many, or ineffective, control systems. Such systems of check and control normally help an organization keep abreast of what is happening, what trends may be observed, and so on; they are feedback systems, and many of them are useful. But many others become meaningless. Some even accomplish the opposite of what they were designed to do. Workers, foremen, middle-management personnel, and even top managers find ways to circumvent the system while acknowledging its existence and paying lip service to it. McGregor and others have noted and documented this phenomenon.

In sum: The manager who can listen creatively is, in an applied sense, an artist. He has opened his mind to the impressions, facts, and sensations of his human, organizational milieu. He has put himself in a position coolly to utilize what he learns: not through translation of impressions and concepts into artistic form and design, but through application of his knowledge and experience to achieve good, original decisions.

Half the battle—awareness We have mentioned the listening-bred awareness that aids good management. This awareness of itself supplies one other clue to the sense and meaning of creative listening. It forms the base on which the executive or manager can build creative decision making.

A dictionary defines awareness as the state of having knowledge, of being cognizant, informed, alert, sophisticated. Inherent in that definition lies the assumption that the aware person has become attuned to his surroundings, including the human element in them, in such a way that he can relate accurately to them. Such awareness or "attunedness" also accomplishes four other main effects, all geared closely to the process of listening and managing creatively:

■ It furnishes the insights that tell the manager *when* a need for creative decision making has developed.

Awareness in this connection serves an alarm-clock function. Before creativity enters into the solution of a problem, and often before a problem has identified itself, the manager must realize that a need for decision exists. Some authorities on creativity go so far as to include this process of *recognition* as the first phase of creation itself. But others treat it separately.

Cases could be cited endlessly to illustrate how listening-induced awareness has informed a manager of a need requiring creative decision. A bank executive launched a thorough revamping of his firm's methods of training junior executives. He had obtained feedback information indicating that current methods were actually causing heavy turnover among trainees. A vice-president, production, of a manufacturing firm sponsored publication of a series of detailed articles after learning, by listening, that production employees "had no idea" of the company's real policies on incentive pay. The articles answered real questions in workers' minds.

■ With awareness the manager knows from moment to moment to what stage his creative process has advanced.

He knows, in brief, where he stands. He knows whether he is researching and preparing, whether he is incubating, or whether he is approaching the moment of illumination. He understands when he is backtracking to gain further data and when he is combining and rejecting possible alternatives. Most importantly, he knows when he has hit upon the "right answer."

■ True awareness can outline for the manager *what* the creative process can be expected to accomplish in reference to a specific problem.

This "blueprinting" aspect of awareness has crucial importance. The manager seeking new ways to eliminate production bottlenecks may find his range of choices for decision making covering a broad spectrum from poor supervision to faulty organization. If he chooses the wrong alternative, the wrong place at which to open the dam, he may further complicate an already complex problem. If he chooses several alternatives, to be launched *seriatim,* he will want the order of the moves specified according to circumstances he understands primarily from listening. He will want to know how far to go in a given task—when to stop.

■ Awareness aids in confident decision making that abides no self-consciousness.

Knowing where he is and what he is doing at each stage in reference to a specific problem; understanding the need for decisiveness or firmness as well as creativity in decision making; and brooking no deterrent to good decisions, the aware listener-manager moves ahead without fear or self-consciousness. His awareness armors him with certainty. It even lets him inhibit the movement of the conscious mind, when that is called for, so that the nonconscious can operate.

Creative listening creates creativity We have discussed the development of creativity in yourself, the manager, and awareness as a stepping-stone to such creativity. Listening-based awareness can play another role. It can suggest to you ways in which you can encourage the creativity of others around you. Creative listening here moves from development of personal skill or competence to establishment of two types of platforms for others' creativity:

- Provision of a creativity-oriented atmosphere
- Provision of specific opportunities for creativity

How this works can be illustrated best by examples. In one case a worker known as a troublemaker suggested an idea. A listening, aware manager picked it up, saw it had value, and put it into effect. The worker suggested another idea—and another. In each case he either saw action or received an explanation of why the idea was impracticable. He came slowly "around" to a more procompany stance. He ceased to be a troublemaker. Ideas poured from him, and many of them had value.

Managers and executives may in many ways dance to a drumbeat different from the worker's. But they are as human as he. They respond to inspiration or encouragement from the outside just as he does.

What does the aware, listening manager *do* to achieve such a result? He may do any of several dozen different things—some of them so apparently trifling as not to deserve attention. Yet they do deserve attention—close attention. They rank among the sweetest fruits of awareness in listening. They include these methods of establishing a creativity-oriented atmosphere or specific opportunities for creativity:

- Recognition of a previously unrecognized and unused skill, ability, or potential. In a chance conversation a manager learns that a fellow manager has a talent for design. He comments that The Boss is looking for someone to design an unusual ashtray to be made out in the shop for the consumer market. The colleague makes the design and receives The Boss's praise for his outstanding work.

- Provision of a pressure-free opportunity. An engineer wanted a chance to think out a problem alone. An aware, listening Boss told him to "work it out at home for a couple of days." He did, and came up with an excellent innovation.

- Allowing or encouraging a person to seek achievement in his own way. A foreman asked for permission to experiment with some novel human relations techniques. An aware, listening department manager gave him a go-ahead.

- Giving specific recognition to ideas or achievement. "A plant improvement suggested by members of the coil winding department," reads the inscription on a product display board in one electronic components manufacturing concern.

- Voicing approval in one area to encourage creativity in another. "You did a terrific job on that lathe, Tom," says the aware manager. "Now I wonder if we're ready to tackle that punch press."

Many more such provocative ways of unearthing creativity could be listed. Each involves a sensitive and alert—an aware—kind of listening and managing, or guiding and directing. Each involves response.

Add a lot of you A final additive goes into managerial creativity based on listening. You. A lot of it.

As your listening acquires the sheen of professionalism, the addition of the You element will come easily and naturally. Decisions will flow more readily "out of your mind." They will belong to no one else because you are now acting as the unique individual that you are. The range of innovation that you can achieve by consciously pursuing creativity will grow, enlarge. Such enlargement will take place around you as well as within you. You will influence others.

In making these statements it is apparent that we are flying directly in the face of the school that maintains that creativity cannot be learned, that an individual is born with it or he does not possess it. We maintain the contrary. Specifically, we hold that every individual, and in particular those with managerial or executive talents, has some creativity. By following certain prescriptions, and in particular by learning to listen, he can develop that creativity and then innovate—turn the creativity into reality. Students of creative endeavor tell us that creative intelligence is compounded of many talents, many skills. Heredity or other factors may set limits on those skills, but within these limitations learning can extend and develop an individual's competence.

What prescription must a manager follow to make his particular brand of listening-bred creativity into reality? Some "do's" may point the way to the more specific material on listening's "how-to's" that will come later. These general guidelines suggest ways in which the injection of the creative You element may be made simpler *before you engage in listening* and after, while chewing over the informational fruits of your listening.

1. *DO relax—you're not on candid camera.* Creative listening and creative managing are done best where the mind's eye is not blinded by the smoke and dust of disruptive tension or passion. Practicing relaxation, thus, means simply retaining mental clarity, allowing thought processes to operate unhindered. Interpersonal communication and creation itself both benefit. For some managers and executives, relaxation may involve reduction of tension arising from fear of taking risks, anxiety, dependence upon authority—even from excessive motivation. In the latter case the manager "tries too hard" and "goes tight." A deliberate mental effort may be required to achieve creativity expressive of the inner You.

2. *DO set yourself in a working frame of mind.* Again, the discharge of effort takes place most effectively where the subject has conditioned himself to exert that effort. The public speaker rehearses, imagines himself before the audience. The football star becomes "keyed up" before the big game. These are working frames of mind for special endeavors. Listening that aims at You-characterized decision making is carried out best when the mental "set" is the appropriate one.

3. *DO attempt to think and talk about familiar things dif-*

ferently. Experiments have shown that we may become chained to habitual thought patterns that inhibit new discoveries, new ideas. Making the effort to think in a new way, even to talk differently, about the things with which we are dealing may break those chains. New combinations of factors may appear: completely original solutions to old, familiar problems. Even renaming might help. To call the furnace room by a different name—Room X, for example—may release a new view of its utility value and its relationship to the other parts of a building. In or after a listening exchange the mental wheels may be turning continually to find new handles for things. In the process the mind strips a particular "thing" of inhibiting associations and looks at it in a fresh way. We can do the same with people of course; Joe the Griper can become Joe the Idea Man, as we have seen.

4. *DO remember that the old may guide but shouldn't control.* You are striking out into relatively uncharted territory every time you attempt to decide creatively. In the process what has gone before, or been done before, by you or others, should serve more as a starting point than as a goalpost or target. Even logic and reason may become less useful, at least in the early stages of creation, no matter how functional they may be as forces holding the organization together. Logic and reason come into greatest play in the verification stage, to "deduce consequences, detect and plug loopholes and point the source, need and nature of supporting details."[2] The old, in short, should not be allowed to act as a brake. The phrase "old brain" has been used to denote thinking that depends too much on the traditional, the accepted or acceptable, the habitual, the already done. In creative listening effort should be directed toward minimization of old brain.

How do you know when the old has intruded to block creativity? It may not always be possible. But the old as block becomes most recognizable when it identifies itself in reference to a new problem in such terms as "this is how it should be,

---

[2] John W. Haefele, *Creativity and Innovation,* copyright © 1962 by Reinhold Publishing Corporation, used by permission of Van Nostrand Reinhold Company.

or has been." This suggests that any new solution must fall into an old mold. The task of adding You can take on difficult, even unpleasant overtones. The manager becomes an analogue of Rebecca of Daphne du Maurier's novel. "I succeeded a man who had been on the job as department manager for twenty-seven years," one manager told me. "Every time I tried to make a move, even when no one said anything, I could feel the pressure. It was as if the ghost of Old Al were guiding me, forcing my hand. 'Al wouldn't have done it that way,' people told me; I listened to them, took my own counsel, and went on doing it my way. Sometimes my way coincided with Al's way."

5. *DO back down when it means moving ahead.* Adding your personal touch and talent will never, under this rule, absolutely require forward action. Creativity may require backtracking in some cases. It may convince you that a backward step will accomplish more good than a positive, forward one. William Foote Whyte tells of the following case:

> John Gossett, vice-president of the Chicago plant of Inland Steel Container Corporation, came to the Chicago plant in 1944, at a time when the Steel Workers Union had the plant under near-total control. Disorganization and demoralization were rampant. "The foremen all seemed on the verge of quitting. The union, with its slowdowns and stoppages and department and plant-wide meetings seemed to be in control of the factory. Even in the period of wartime prosperity, the plant was losing money. Gossett decided that the first job was to stiffen the back of management."
>
> Stiffen it he did. He refused to discuss *anything* with the union outside of grievance meetings. In retaliation, the union hurled grievance after grievance at a harassed management. Tension built up. Several workers were suspended when, on union orders, they refused to follow management instructions involving a change in their working schedule. In all, 53 workers were suspended; the plant was forced to close. It remained closed for nine weeks "while the (work schedule) case was argued before an arbitrator." Less than three months later the plant closed again for 191 days, beginning with a three week

industry-wide steel strike. Management began to look at the possibility that it would have to shut the plant permanently.

All this time middle management personnel and foremen had borne the brunt of the pressure from above: they were the men in the middle who carried Gossett's hard-nosed policies to the level of the work floor. But finally, after some three years, Gossett's assistant, Novy, went in and "laid it on the line." He told Gossett bluntly that the morale of the management organization was very low, that Gossett's autocratic approach had the members of management up in arms against him, that if Gossett did not change his ways even more serious problems could be expected.

Gossett backtracked. For a whole day he listened to the complaints that others in management had against him. "Not once did he argue and when each finished Gossett thanked him for his full expression of feeling. From this point on, John Gossett was a different man in the plant." [3]

Backing down may, in other words, amount to facing facts. It happens all the time where a manager learns by listening and proceeds to his decision with no sense of compulsion that he *must* act in accord with earlier models or standards, even his own.

A word of caution is in order. The manager who *repeatedly* reverses direction should look to his laurels. He may be making decisions on the basis of inadequate information. He certainly runs the risk of joining the fits-and-starts school of management.

6. *DO use checklists where they appear appropriate.* They have been decried as crutches, but they can provide a take-off point for deep, serious mental effort. And the manager using them need not confine himself to the items on his checklist exclusively: the bottom of the last page of a checklist may be the point at which creativity really begins. Look, for example, at the widely used product checklist developed by Alex Osborn:

---

[3] William F. Whyte, *Money and Motivation*, Harper & Row, Publishers, Incorporated, New York, 1955, pp. 99–109.

Put to other uses? New ways to use as is? Other uses if modified?

Adapt? What else is like this? What other ideas does this suggest? Does the past offer parallels? What could I copy? Whom could I emulate?

Modify? New twist? Change meaning, color, motion, odor, form, shape? Other changes?

Magnify? What to add? More time? Greater frequency? Stronger? Larger? Thicker? Extra value? Plus ingredient? Duplicate? Multiply? Exaggerate?

Minify? What to substitute? Smaller? Condensed? Miniature? Lower? Shorter? Lighter? Omit? Split up? Understate?

Substitute? Who else instead? What else instead? Other ingredients? Other material? Other process? Other power? Other place? Other approach? Other tone of voice?

Rearrange? Interchange components? Other pattern? Other layout? Other sequence? Transpose cause and effect? Change pace? Change schedule?

Reverse? Transpose positive and negative? How about opposites? Turn it backward? Turn it upside down? Reverse roles? Change shoes? Turn tables? Turn other cheek?

Combine? How about a blend, an alloy, an assortment, an ensemble? Combine units? Combine purposes? Combine appeals? Combine ideas?[4]

7. *DO keep your concrete goal firmly and determinedly in mind.* You are not pursuing creativity per se; it doesn't exist in the abstract. You *are* pursuing creativity in specific reference to a problem or situation. In this pursuit you will want to recognize and understand organizational realities: capabilities as well as shortcomings, advantages as well as disadvantages. Which realities will weigh more heavily in your accounting as you pass through the early stages of creation will depend on the circumstances.

> Nearly every manufacturing plant and many offices have their "monster in the back room"—a piece of equipment that workers fear and even hate. The piece of equipment often represents a new departure for the company—a new 360 computer, a

[4] Alex F. Osborn, *Applied Imagination*, Charles Scribner's Sons, New York, 1957, p. 318.

new in-house printing press, a continuous operation paper-making machine. But because the human ground was not creatively considered and prepared in advance, workers see it as a threat, an engine of technological displacement. In most such cases resistance could have been minimized by listening to possible objections and answering them before installation. Creative decision making could have taken into account the widespread inclination among all of us to view new things with suspicion—and found communications ways to allay that suspicion.

The New Result

Now we can see where it all leads, this creativity in listening and managing: to the release of productive and creative energies that makes for outstanding performance.

No single, simple formula for achievement of the goal exists. That cannot be; for we are not working with formulas. We are trying to understand that fluid method of invention called the creative process. We are trying to utilize it with listening so that we can understand the ways in which innovation is produced and made effective. To do this the manager must first understand and adjust, must tailor, must comprehend the shape of the group and individual minds with which he is working. He listens to create better.

Listening, the search for the new and more perfectly adapted—these can join and become a way of life. Unless he makes the effort to join them, the manager or executive may, in effect, be denying both himself and the people around him the right of creative participation.

The manager who can make the creative listening approach an article of faith has taken a long step. He is committed to both creativity and listening. He has started down the road to the untrodden and even unknown. And that is creativity's great beauty.

5
Preparation — Mental, Emotional, and Physical

> Shapes of all sizes, great and small,
> That stood along the floor and by the wall,
> And some loquacious vessels were; and some
> Listen'd perhaps, but never talked at all.
> —Rubaiyat of Omar Khayyam

"I don't advise you," said Clarence Randall, "to start talking until you have started thinking. It's no good opening the tap if there's nothing in the tank."

Similarly, it serves only a limited purpose to start listening before you have made certain that your mental and emotional makeup does not betray or nullify your listening efforts. Where that happens, understanding is not achieved, and understanding is the name of the listening game.

> Two executives, members of the eastern headquarters staff of a major corporation, were discussing ways to develop better coordination between key departments.

"Do you think you could persuade Art that he ought to check his reports out with us before finalizing them?" asked one man.

The other bristled visibly. "Art's doing fine and I wish people would stop throwing rocks at him," the second executive said. Because he was offended, this second man at that point ceased to take an effective part in the conversation. He withdrew, psychologically, from the discussion. The conversation had to be terminated soon after—without effective resolution.

The second executive stopped listening when an assistant's name was mentioned. Yet it had not been the intention of the other man to rattle or bait him or to open any skeleton-filled closets. The first man made that clear to me when I asked him about it later. "I just forgot how sensitive Joe has become on the subject of Art recently," I was told.

In this actual case an executive allowed an emotional reaction to cloud his intellect. He lost effectiveness immediately. We all share in greater or less degree the thinking fault of the second executive. Is there a man who can say he never refused admittance to a word or an idea in its pure form? Is there anyone who can say his mind never rose in revolt at something said by another? These are twin embarrassments of our age. "Let us stop shouting at one another," pleaded President Richard M. Nixon. What he meant was: "Let us begin to listen —really listen—to one another."

So it is a matter of degree. But those who suffer from it in greater degree, those to whom it occurs often, have not done their disciplinary homework; they will find their communications limping. They have, most simply, not cleared away the mental and emotional underbrush that can render useless a listening effort.

The penultimate work of preparation for listening centers mainly on the recognition and elimination of mental and emotional inhibitors of understanding; on the enumeration of those words and concepts that we are unable to accept as they come to us or that arouse us to wrath or indignation or other emotion. Such recognition and elimination take us to the heart of the meaning of language. If words, ideas, and concepts can fall at the doors of our minds, if they can set fire to what should be an orderly thought structure, then language impedes or interferes with clear communication. Language becomes less useful. Words will fail to "come through" to the listener's mind or they will penetrate in garbled form or they will ignite emotion: in any of these cases the accurate transmission of information becomes difficult or impossible.

Yet we depend on spoken language as a primary mode of communication. We have no adequate substitute for it. We are trying to give language its full validity as we search out our own and others' emotion arousers or the barriers that refuse admittance to ideas.

Perhaps the first question to ask, and answer, is: What happened inside the second executive's mind to make him bridle and then lose effectiveness in a conversation that had proceeded smoothly prior to the chance mention of a man's name?

MIND AND EMOTION: BLOCKS AND FILTERS

What happened is what happens so often in every life context. An emotional filter slipped between the words delivered by the first man and the mind of the second man. The filter was inside the second executive's head; he took umbrage because he felt that Art, one of his subordinates, was being unjustly criticized. Yet that had not happened at all.

What was the *reason* for what happened? We have to guess to some extent because we cannot open the executive's brain, nor can we lay his emotional makeup out on a table and examine it under a microscope. What we can assume is that the executive had become oversensitive to criticism of Art because he felt it reflected on him as a manager. Or similar past experiences had made the executive's life difficult. Or the executive's own background and environment had built in him a defensive posture that make him quick to arouse.

This is a filter: a reaction that in one way or another, for one reason or another, changes what is heard, gives it new, and false, meaning, and in the end works on an emotion to distort the sense of the message.

A parallel phenomenon is the mental block: the habit of mind, or attitude, or belief that omits or deletes all or part of what is said, or that edits it so that it enters the mind meaning something different from what was intended.

Accurate transmission of information, it has been said, depends on three things, each indispensable:

A sender

A message

A receiver

The listening manager cannot directly, immediately, and conclusively control the first and second ingredients. He can control the third: his own mind, his own emotions.

Filters: Transmuting Gold into Base Metal

Emotional filters do not simply tune out a word, a phrase, an idea, and substitute something different for what is heard. They bring emotion into play as a destructive or constructive force. All too often, the emotion is negative; it twists beyond recognition a whole subject, an entire conversation, a series of ideas from a particular speaker. A speech can fail totally to impart information.

Operating in this negative way, filters transmute the gold of the message into base metal. At this point the message can no longer carry its true, deserved weight in the listener's thinking. It performs an entirely different function: to serve an emotional end in the listener's interior world. Misunderstanding ensues, and this, as Theodor Reik tells us, is worse than not to understand. Not understanding at all, we are at least open to clarification and explanation. Misunderstanding, we charge off into the dark, thinking we know where we are going.

Filters produce emotional response simply because each of us *feels* strongly or emotionally about certain things. The emotions aroused may be positive or negative, as noted; and if positive they may not be harmful. The subordinate who, after a talk with The Boss, finds himself eager to do battle for the company may be reacting emotionally. The emotion, triggered by a filter that interpreted something—or many things—The Boss said, may not carry the man far or long. Yet it cannot be said to be immediately harmful.

Even so, there exists a danger here. The same man who roars with enthusiasm after a talk with The Boss is all too often the same one whose spirits can be dashed by a poorly chosen word. And dashed illogically, by the heat of unnecessary emotion.

The filters producing negative responses are the ones to sort out and guard against. They result from stereotyped reactions, from misconceptions, from prejudices. Our frames of reference, the signs and guidelines by which we form impressions and judgments, have become fixed. The man who "flies by stereotype" will find it difficult or impossible to listen because his understanding will trip constantly over the built-in filters that set off his emotional reactions. He may lose control of his emotions. A subordinate mentions that Sales has been given for study a copy of a new plan for advertising the company's products. "Why?" thunders The Boss. "Why Sales? They'll just foul it up!" The Boss's mind has closed with a slam, propelled by destructive anger. He is no longer listening.

Blocks That Don't Build

If we consider mental blocks to be attitudes, or mental habits, or beliefs, we can see how destructive they can be. They simply refuse admittance to certain words or phrases, ideas or concepts. What comes through to the listener's mind is (1) nothing, or (2) something entirely different from what was intended.

Emotion need not be involved where blocks are concerned. Mention "incentive" to a worker and he or she, if trained in a certain school, may simply read "exploitation" or "exploitative system of payment" into the place where the word "incentive" appeared. The word incentive simply stops at the threshold of the worker's mind; what comes through is a negative dilution on the order of "another company gimmick to get more work for less pay."

Other words and ideas on which mental blocks hinge abound in the business context. The phrase, "cooperation with the union," draws a total blank in some managerial circles. The possibility of such cooperation is simply rejected, or is translated into a concept such as "manipulation." "Efficiency" has been found, among workers, to suffer from a stigma similar to that of "incentive." The word "listening" itself may encounter a mental block. Without thinking beyond the basic meaning of the word, without attempting to view listening as one of the Four Horsemen of Communication, many a manager or executive simply refuses entry to the thought that listening can be multidirectionally useful. He may see listening as something you practice only when in the presence of a superior. Superior-subordinate listening is excluded entirely.

Every manager can draw up a list of mental blocks that he has encountered in others. He will know them by their effects: they prevent full or accurate understanding and in the end have direct, negative bearing on the individual's understanding and subsequent behavior.

Like emotional filters, a major problem with our own mental blocks is that they may have such deep roots that we cannot identify all of them. In such a case the difficulty of locating them is simply compounded.

Identifying stereotypes In the last analysis blocks and filters both develop because stereotypes have grown up. We may end up classifying an individual as belonging to a single group and as possessing all the basic attributes or characteristics of that group. Or we may write off a new idea because it jars against a pet prejudice. Or we may never give a company system a full chance to operate because "I've seen this type of thing before and it never works."

People stereotypes work, perhaps, the greatest harm. They may exclude from the listening orbit of the manager or executive a whole class or group. "You can't talk to a chemist." "Why try to deal with a union man?" These are group stereotypes, people stereotypes. They ignore the fact that every person fulfills many roles in life, that each of us can be put into a number of pigeonholes: fathers, husbands, workers, neighbors, automobile owners, taxpayers, churchgoers, sportsmen. Women play the same multiplicity of roles. Both sexes play many roles that have not been mentioned here.

The problem is that our inferences about any individual may be based on a single role or frame of perception. To use family, recreational, occupational, dress or clothing, residence, or other single characteristic as the clue that gives us a label for another person bespeaks poor and misleading thinking. Such a practice can never help us really identify and classify another in depth. It ignores the differences in people. It does not take into consideration the reality that from one point in time to another each of us is different.

There is no denying that stereotypes serve as quick communicators. They serve this purpose in business and industry as in communication in general. But we have to recognize that they are half-meaningless and can be totally dysfunctional: listening falters because understanding falters.

Examples of common organizational stereotypes and their accompanying filters and blocks could be cited endlessly. Many of them fall into clearly definable categories, and can be enumerated:

"THING" STEREOTYPES:

- "That new lathe has never been any good," notes a worker angrily, voicing a view widely held in his department. The lathe actually does not perform up to expectations; the workers see to that. Their belief leads to inefficient operation.

- "We've never believed that those work savers could help us," says an executive, "and we're not going to change now." He refuses a request that the company get a work saver even on a trial basis and workers go on using human power to move heavy loads. The workers remain angry.

GROUP STEREOTYPES:

- "They put a girl on this job—it was bound to be fouled up," says a personnel man. A man is assigned to the job and eleven eligible and competent women feel downgraded, frustrated, angry.

■ "Give an industrial engineer half a chance and he'll ruin morale in your department before you can say 'get out,'" says a department manager. He refuses legitimate IE aid and the productivity of his entire department suffers.

SYSTEM STEREOTYPES:

■ "I've never seen the quality control system that did any good," gripes a plant manager. His efforts to install such a system, by order of higher headquarters, fail because they are halfhearted.

■ "Give me the old forms any day," says the director of purchasing. He fails to listen to suggestions for an improved, simplified form.

Stereotyping leads to rigidity, to inflexibility. Free, open communication in a listening atmosphere cannot take place because some, or many, doors are closed. Stereotyping is the enemy of creativity, a key goal of listening. And creativity is the father of innovation.

> The new vice-president of a multiplant furniture manufacturing firm in the Southwest had had some unfortunate experiences with work forces made up partly of Spanish-speaking employees. On one occasion, in a previous job, he had seen a whole department of Mexican-Americans sit down and threaten to walk out if a suspended worker was not reinstated. In another case a group of Spanish-speaking workers had failed in a body to appear for Saturday overtime. The vice-president ascribed it all to their "Latin temperament" and acquired a deep-seated distaste for all workers whose mother tongue was Spanish.
>
> The Veep's new company had one plant that was not performing as well as it might have—as well as it had only a year earlier. The Veep learned quickly that the plant had a large complement of Spanish-speaking workers. He immediately made up his mind that the problems of the underachieving plant could be solved only by closing the plant.
>
> The Veep made a lightning inspection of the problem plant to confirm his long-range estimate. He returned to headquarters

saying, "We've got only one way to go—close it." And eventually the company did "spin off" the one plant. It was purchased by another firm that took it over, established a personnel department with a Spanish-speaking assistant, launched a communications program in English and Spanish—and in a few months put the plant on its productivity feet.

In a situation demanding creative approaches and solutions, the Veep had made a decision based on a stereotype, a prejudice. He "gave away" a perfectly good operation.

The cure of stereotypes Can stereotypes and their typical offspring, blocks and filters, be cured—uprooted? Many of them can. Nichols and Stevens in their fine study listed three ways to attack your own "word barriers" or "labels that hinder listening":

1. Make every effort to become aware of the words (or ideas) that upset you emotionally. It is often a good idea in this word-identification process to make a written list of them.

2. Once identified, the words should be analyzed. Why do they affect you as they do? Was the acquisition of the words accomplished on a logical basis? Has an effort ever been made to see all sides of the situations to which the words have been applied as labels? And, most important of all, have the situations behind the words changed so that the words are no longer applicable?

3. Rationalize the impact that such words have upon you by discussing them freely with other people.[1]

What about mental blocks? They do not set up the red flag of an emotional reaction. They simply exclude all or part of an idea or concept. Inevitably, their identification is more difficult.

Some signs can, however, tell you when you have blocks that are hindering clear thinking—and reducing your operational effectiveness. Blocks may exist if you can answer any of these questions in the affirmative:

■ Do you find your thoughts and reactions on some subjects or areas of your operation falling into a rigid pattern?

[1] Ralph G. Nichols and Leonard A. Stevens, *Are You Listening?* McGraw-Hill Book Company, New York, 1957, p. 102.

- Are you hearing good news only—and very little bad?
- In your view are your associates—subordinates, primarily—living up to their creative potential? If not, the fault may lie with you, with your inability to *accept* newness.
- Are your associates given to what you would consider stereotyped thinking—and have you made efforts to control such stereotyped thinking, to open the channels of creativity, added responsibility, innovation?
- Do your methods of operation with your associates appear to strangle new ideas? Is the meeting every Monday morning at 10 A.M. a weekly bore, unproductive and wearing?
- Is it within your capacity, and the capacity of your team, to ask *why?* Or *how?* Or *how else?*
- Do you hear from your people too much about problems solved and jobs completed, too little about problems or plans involving people, customers, products, and so on?
- Is your team able to review interrogatively, or to rethink, decisions already made?
- Do you see too many projects falling apart and having to be discarded?

A yes on any of these questions should suggest the need for careful analysis.

You as blockbuster As you listen, truly listen, more and better, you may find that your own relative freedom from stereotypes and prejudices, from blocks and filters, helps eradicate the blocks and filters that hamper others' thinking and listening. At the least you will not be reinforcing those blocks and prejudices.

> The new director of manufacturing of a chemical company visited one of the company's plants for the first time. He talked with managers, foremen, and small groups of workers from each department of the plant. The workers in one area had one major gripe: to operate one of the mixing kettles in one building, the worker assigned to the controls had to stand outside the building in a makeshift canvas "cage" that provided almost no protection against the weather in winter. The duty was rotated regularly, but in winter the operator always suffered

from the cold. The system was time-honored, part of the plant scene, according to local management, and bothered no one abnormally.

The manufacturing director learned differently while listening to plant workers and shop stewards. The workers had reacted to management's hard attitude on the subject—to management's own mental block—by erecting their own emotional filter. They spoke to the new director of manufacturing in impassioned terms. Mere mention of the cage angered them.

The director visited "the cage." It was cold outside, and the operator was seriously uncomfortable even though he wore heavy winter clothing.

The director left. A week later he had obtained an appropriation to build an enclosed cage that would be as warm as the inside of the plant. He asked the plant manager to have the installation put in as quickly as possible. When the job was done, he returned to the plant and talked again with personnel from all parts of the plant. The atmosphere had become pleasanter; attitudes among the workers had softened. Even the plant manager thanked him for the decision. This director of manufacturing became a blockbuster. His own preparation, his own skill at listening without allowing another's stereotypes to control his thinking, had sucked the emotion out of an explosive situation. He had eliminated a major labor problem, one with connotations that went far beyond the confines of the department.

Preparation for listening through elimination of blocks and filters, through recognition of stereotypes, should involve some further steps.

■ *You will not want to leave a vacuum in your mind where blocks and filters have been removed.* On the contrary, more broadly based views will be substituted for the hard, frozen, narrow ones that produced the blocks and filters. Things will be seen as they are, in round perspective, not flat. Spanish-speaking workers will be accepted as individuals and as workers, with ambitions, drives, and desires similar to those of workers from other minority and majority groups. Spanish-speaking workers may, of course, be seen as having special cultural and language problems; this need not do violence to the basic concept of them as individuals and workers. Here the half-truth of a group stereotype merely gives way to the whole truth that a man is an individual and a human being, different from all others.

■ *In eradicating your own blocks and filters, those of others will stand out more clearly, but you will resist the temptation to attack them directly.* Going over to the attack in such instances only reinforces the other's stereotypes; it forces the other to argue in defense of his position. Attacking misconceptions, or false ideas, or blocks and filters, say psychiatrists, undermines the other's self-image. In fighting to maintain that self-image he may strengthen the false concept, the stereotype, the misconception. He certainly becomes less the listener and more the blind defender. When The Boss says, "These foremen are all alike—goof-offs," he will only defend the statement more strenuously if you force him to argue in defense of his statement. But if you say, "Some of them may be, sir, but a lot of others ought to stay on the team—and we can build on them," The Boss may see some light. He may start listening.

■ *You will, in cleaning out the underbrush of your own mind, prepare to climb more readily into the frame of reference of others in the organization to the degree compatible with your relationship with them and with the time necessarily involved in getting to know them.* Here we touch on readiness to "empathize" in listening, not on the process of empathy itself. We touch on preparedness to know others from the inside, to see things as they see them and to know and feel things as they know and feel them. Once our own tendency to judge quickly, superficially, and falsely is gone, or reduced, we should have increased our ability to step into the other's mental shoes. The Boss no longer stands as a cigar-chewing automaton who wants everyone to work until 7 P.M.; he becomes a human being with human characteristics. The subordinate ceases to be a work dodger who disappears out the door at 4:30 P.M., and becomes a worried man with a sick wife.

■ *Your own laborious housecleaning should teach you ways patiently to plant ideas so that they can take root, grow, and displace others' blocks and filters.* Patience must guide the hand and mind of him who would influence others in any way; and influencing others in the organization so that they will listen better, communicate better, without the destructive impedimenta of blocks and filters, is part of the manager's job. It is part of the way he gets things done through others. Everyone has seen organizations where one or several men keep bringing reason and a new view to meetings through patient, filter-free, block-free discussion, including listening. I personally have had the pleasure of watching one such man in action. He used the "hypothesis approach" masterfully. "What if—," he would say. Or: "I wonder if we could—." He continually elicited creative response.

■ *You will see ways to reach others, with a view to eradicating or reducing their destructive blocks and filters, their stereotypes, by working through their leaders, their organizations, the things they admire or like.* In one plant a small group of workers, all Roman Catholics, met annually for an Easter breakfast. Six months after a new plant manager was assigned, Easter came around; the group invited him as a matter of course. They had done the same for his predecessor for years, and no one had ever showed up. But the new man went. He listened, and learned a lot; he also reached the group with the special message that he couldn't be written off as the all-business, couldn't-care-less type of manager. His action in attending the breakfast spoke more loudly than words against the unfortunate antimanagement stereotypes of some in the group.

■ *You will understand that the action method of listening, the creative method we are describing, will do more to remove blocks and filters in others than almost anything else you can do.* Good listening, we have said, involves acceptance of the other's statements, of his person, of his dignity. Of his prejudices and misconceptions, even; of his blocks and filters. Of *him*. How often has a worker stormed into a foreman's office, had a chance to speak his entire piece, and gone away mollified and even slightly changed, his problems obliterated by the mere fact that his foreman listened to him? Many firms today teach their foremen, managers, and executives listening just so they can soften harsh attitudes in this way while communicating better.

Influence or manipulate? Can we utilize the stereotypes and prejudices of others in such a way as to communicate better, influence those others, and gain benefit from their stereotypes?

It's done all the time. Unions, for example, send Negro organizers to plants with large Negro populations. Many companies appoint Polish, or Irish, or Italian managers to plants with heavy representations of those nationalities. One company makes it a policy to appoint personnel men of the appropriate national origin to its plants in a Puerto Rican area of New York City, in Montreal, and in a heavily Germanic area of the Midwest.

One caveat: A factor of manipulation enters into the equation where the effort to take advantage of prejudices, misconceptions, or stereotypes is made primarily to manipulate and not to communicate better. A manager, or a company, may make the mistake of devoting so much attention to capitalizing on stereotypes that he forgets his prime task—to listen, understand, and seek to influence honestly, on the basis of what he really thinks, knows, and *is*. The latter has a far broader base in reality and represents a much more attainable goal.

Attempts to manipulate, rather than communicate, are based in intellectual dishonesty and may lead to misrepresentation, exaggeration, distortion—all the many and varied perpetrations of the propagandist. The manager who joins his superior's club and then "butters up" The Boss may, if found to be inefficient on the job, fall farther and faster than the man who attends strictly to duty. The foreman who, on starting work, first looks for mistakes made by the foreman on the shift before him—to cover his own inadequacies—will soon or eventually find himself in the cold, harsh glare of a blunder that he cannot cover up.

PLANNING EXTENDS TO THE PHYSICAL

Preparation may extend, finally, into the physical arena. When an occasion for listening is known to be approaching, some review of where and how that occasion will be held, dealt with, or handled is nearly always called for. Study of the goals of the listening exercise, and of the format of the exercise in relation to those goals, will be imperative.

Consider some questions in relation to meetings, perhaps the most common—and most maligned—type of group listening occasion. Will the meeting be routine, with no possibility of creative input? Will it be exploratory or problem-oriented? Will it be reportorial? Will it share some or all of these characteristics? Will it have other characteristics?

With those questions answered, others must be asked. How long will the meeting last? Where will it be held? Who will attend? When will it begin? What will be needed to conduct it?

Because listening is demanding and difficult, and because preparation cannot extend too far, still other questions may be asked. For example: Who might be brought into the listening exercise, the meeting, after it ends? Who might be brought into it before it begins?

> Phil, the manager of an electronics plant, used question-answer sessions with employees as a deliberately arranged means of listening. Before each session he went over the possible questions he might hear and the possible answers he ought to give. He conducted this review with department managers and foremen shortly before his sessions with workers. In this way he minimized the occasions on which he had to speak "off the cuff" on a completely "local" or departmental subject. His preparation closed possible traps in advance; it also assured that departmental management teams and he were on the same wavelength as regards key questions of policy and planning.
>
> Phil had one other technique for use in the rare situations where workers rose in meetings with unexpected questions. When he encountered such questions, Phil said frankly, "I don't know the answer to that, but I'll get it and make sure it gets back to you."
>
> In these meetings Phil developed an *esprit* in his work force that showed on the work floor in steadily improving productivity figures and profit and loss statements. He counted every minute of preparation for such listening occasions as well spent. He employed a simple philosophy and some simple guidelines that any manager can follow.

Brushup

Phil respected his workers: this was his philosophy. He did not meet with them to "put them on" or "snow" them. He wanted them to *know*. His brushup preparation made it inevitable that he would in his employee Q and A sessions nearly always reveal a phenomenal grasp of facts and statistics, even of names and dates. He had a full, up-to-date picture of each department's situation as regards working conditions, future plans, the progress of current programs, and the details of group performance. He had four main purposes in mind:

1. In his advance briefings he wanted to listen to department managers and foremen *first,* not only to obtain information but also to give due regard to their positions of authority in their own areas, their own suggestions and opinions.

2. He wanted, in the same advance contacts, to bring the foremen and department managers into the listening–decision-making process and to functionalize his own leadership role.

3. He wanted to make sure that he and his managers were on the same wavelength.

4. He wanted to be prepared for his meetings so that he could utilize them most advantageously to:

- Keep workers honestly informed of goals and accomplishments
- Relate individual or small unit efforts to such goals and accomplishments
- Relate the entire work force's efforts to those goals
- Place such information in the context of the plant's performance *results*
- Enable the group to take part in planning and problem solving through contribution of opinion and idea
- Sell, without using that word, the need for higher individual and group effort

How far, O Lord? How far can such preparation for a listening exercise go?

Down to the last pencil, the last pad of yellow paper. Attention to detail marks the successful listener just as it marks the successful genius.

Listening, in fact, thrives best where advance planning for a planned convocation extends even into those gray areas where prediction is difficult: for example, into the choice of a setting whose physical characteristics can have a bearing on success or failure. A meeting with workers may be more productive if held close to the work area. An executive board meeting on a sensitive subject was most profitably held outside the organization's headquarters—at lunch in the conference room of a local restaurant. An office allowing little or no privacy may be the wrong place for a performance review with a subordinate.

Planning, in short, can take account of an element sometimes overlooked in the organization of a group communication exercise: atmosphere. The restaurant conference room exactly accommodated the group of executives who were to attend the meeting; its situation within the restaurant complex gave it an informal association that contributed heavily to the success of the meeting. "It seemed less businesslike, and for that reason it succeeded beyond our expectations," one executive commented afterward. "Everyone contributed, everyone listened."

A safety director never attended a plant meeting—and he held many of them with small groups of workers and foremen —without wearing his distinctive white "hard hat." He took the hat off during the meeting, of course. But its presence in the room served as a reminder that safety, and only safety, comprised the subject matter. His hard hat set the tone of his brief sessions with workers.

A top executive of a major conglomerate made periodic visits to the firm's scattered plants. He believed that informality should keynote these visits. Too much formality, he found, helped give his field visits the sense of top-secret missions during which major decisions had to be reached. To dissipate that feeling he started meeting with plant managers and their key aides in the plant cafeterias, over coffee. His feedback increased tremendously.

Once a year the personnel director in a small plant meets

individually with each of the plant's employees. He holds these meetings on the anniversary of the individual's date of hire. He wants to listen more than talk during the sessions. To set the stage for the meeting he not only peruses the individual's employment record; before the meeting starts he also sets out on his desk a new product, a picture taken in the man's department, or some other visually attractive item that will engage the man's attention and launch a one- or two-minute conversation of a completely neutral nature on a subject about which the individual is or should be informed. "The TLCs (talking-listening conferences) go much better that way," the personnel man notes. "The pressure, if any, drops away and we can just talk. Then I just listen."

Classify and organize Where order rules, where the relationships among various facts or plans or programs are understood in advance by the listener, the listening audience falls much more readily into the spirit of the effort. Conversely, where a would-be listener shows mental or physical disorganization, his listening may fall as flat as the table on which he has to pound to get attention.

Here, attention from the "audience"—the meeting participants—equates with respect. Those to whom you want to listen must respect you or they will feel that words are wasted. You can shout or order an individual to obtain attention; you can command it by the simple force of your position of authority. But attention or respect, naturally and freely paid, makes for the finest kind of listening, the most effective.

Lack of organization and planning accomplishes the opposite: lack of attention. Listening in such a context may be wasted.

> The new department manager believed in "informal" meetings. He would call his area, general, and line foremen together with little warning and virtually no preparation on his own part. Sometimes he would get up and leave the meeting to ransack his desk for notes or statistics; sometimes he failed to find what he was looking for.
>
> The men attending the meetings soon began to chafe. They felt that their time was valuable. What they failed to do during

working hours, they often had to do after the day had ended. They began to find excuses for not attending the meetings even though, at times, they were able to obtain answers and information they needed in their work. What had happened was that the clear sense of disorganization and lack of plan had soured them on the whole departmental meeting process. The curious fact: this department manager, in other contexts, ranked as an excellent listener.

Meetings without meaning are avoidable This is true despite the tongue-in-cheek comments on meetings and committee planning. Who hasn't heard such comments?

"A camel is a horse designed by a committee."

"If you want to get nothing done, form a committee and hold a meeting."

"A conference is a meeting to decide when the next meeting will be held."

"A meeting brings together a group of the unfit, appointed by the unwilling, to do the unnecessary."

"A conference is a meeting of a group of men who singly can do nothing but who collectively agree that nothing can be done."

The reality has nothing to do with such snidery, of course. Meetings and conferences characterize organizational life as almost nothing else can. They have become typical. By audio-visual means such as closed-circuit television, the participants in a meeting can be plugged in from San Francisco, Toronto, Chicago, and Dallas for a meeting chaired in New York City. Here, listening can take place from coast to coast. The conference call is already a highly perfected audio technique for holding a meeting with widely scattered participants.

Whatever the means by which participants are "brought together," meaningless meetings can be avoided. How? Through understanding of their very real, very valuable purposes. These include:

- To coordinate planning and program development
- To encourage group contribution to decision making, both to develop stronger motivation in carrying out the partic-

ipative decision and to assure complete understanding of all that the decision entails

- To dignify decisions by employing consultative methods so that others not in the meeting will respect them more
- To encourage free interpersonal exchange and creativity

In all meetings with one or more of these goals, listening can and should be a functional technique of participation. In preparing a meeting, then, listening should be given its due measure of consideration alongside other, more physical or procedural questions.

We come now to the manner in which such listening—any listening—is done: to what goes on in the listener's mind as he listens.

6
The Fact and the Act of Listening

> I know you believe you understand what you think I said, but I am not sure you realize that what you heard is not what I meant.
> —SIGN IN PENTAGON NEWSROOM

DISSECTION DESTROYS, notes the biologist. So, in a sense, does our analysis of listening. Where we have spoken of a "listening effort," or a "listening project," we have been referring to an identifiable and separable phase of management activity in which interpersonal listening was, or could have been, practiced. We were looking at listening through a microscope.

Yet phases, or practice efforts, should blend into total practice, a habitually applied skill. What we learn in dissection becomes part of our stock of knowledge. We cannot forget that in analyzing we are doing what laboratory dissection does—or a motion picture camera. The camera freezes the action; the baseball pitcher, caught on film, appears to have his arm in an extremely awkward position. The pitcher is nonetheless expert.

So we have to dissect the skill of listening still further to find out what circumstances of mood and method make it succeed. We hesitate to call listening a skill, but no better word offers. Our hesitancy has its roots in the same feeling that disturbed one authority when he discussed skill and human relations in combination. "Human relations," this expert noted, "has a cold-blooded connotation of proficiency, technical expertness, calculated effect."

THE QUALITY OF ENGAGEMENT

Pretend. You are listening now. A man talks. You perpend. You are consciously, actively participating with him in this communications exercise. You are seeking information, ideas, attitudes, emotions. You have the long-range goal of building on your knowledge of things, people, the man in front of you, your organization. You are target-oriented.

A special element goes into this listening if it is to be optimally productive. We call that element *engagement* between listener and listenee. It occurs when the listener is honestly interested in what the other has to say, and the other person realizes it and finds it worthwhile to continue communicating. Listener and listenee mesh.

This is essentially the establishment of what psychiatrists call *rapport*. It has been termed *involvement*. Personnel men seek to achieve it in interviewing, a pure form of listening. As in psychotherapy, the listener tries to set a communications framework in which both parties can feel they are helping solve or resolve a common problem. They may disagree initially or eventually; no matter. The sense of collaboration is there, making possible on the part of the listener what one company has called "deep-sensing."

> The top research chemist in a medium-sized chemical firm came to The Boss, the president, and announced without warn-

ing that he was quitting. The chemist had been with the firm more than five years; he was on the way up, and seemed to enjoy his work. A number of key projects depended on his creative juices for their successful prosecution.

The president took the news calmly, but not so calmly that he brushed the chemist off. He said simply, "I wish you'd take a minute to tell me about it—your reasons."

The chemist began to talk. He listed what have been called the "good" reasons for his decision, but only came to the "real" reasons after some ten minutes of conversation in which he grew more and more reasonable, less and less disturbed. At this point the president had achieved engagement.

The chemist's good reasons for leaving were typical: He felt, mainly, that another company might offer greater advancement potential. His real, or underlying, reasons were also relatively typical. He felt that Stoneman, the vice-president over him, was not giving him the freedom that he needed to conduct what he called "intuitive" research. It became clear to the president, as he listened, that the chemist had rationalized from his sense of frustration to the other "good" reasons he had for quitting. The president asked for and received the chemist's permission to talk to Stoneman.

Discussing the incident with Stoneman later, the president found that the vice-president had no idea that the chemist's feeling of frustration was so strong. The picture changed; Stoneman proved amenable to suggestion; the chemist stayed on his job.

The hunt for idea, suggestion, complaint, interior rationale in such a context becomes an ever-moving, mentally demanding search for underlying truths in an atmosphere of mutual trust and interest. You do not talk down. You try to make sure the other spells out his meanings as he sees them.

Empathy versus Engagement

Is empathy a helpful precondition for good managerial listening, the same as engagement? Not at all. Empathy exists independently in the manager-listener. It can exist before or during—or without—engagement. You can "feel with" another or others without engaging them fully in communication of any kind. Empathy, the emotional-mental stance, will help establish engagement; but engagement, or rapport, can exist alone.

Engagement may be established at the start of a communications exercise or only after effort and a period of time. It may never be achieved in a particular listening situation. A staff meeting may turn into a separation of minds. On the other hand, I have observed meetings at which everyone shouted at everyone else. I honestly felt some of the participants, despite the shouting, were *engaged* with others present. The shouting inhibited real listening, unquestionably. But it was accepted as normal in that company; it did not prevent engagement.

In another situation a business conversation that might have produced valuable truths may fail utterly. The manager of a major department in a U.S. government office told me after talking to his top aide: "I just couldn't get the inputs I wanted out of Mike today. Yet I know he has them." Questioning indicated that the manager had been in a hurry and had not really established engagement. Two men who normally communicated well had wasted more than half an hour. In other cases the difficulty may lie with the listenee—in his inability to think calmly about a particular subject, for example.

Thus it is true: engagement that enables another's meanings to emerge may be impossible because of a flaw in the communications style of either the listener or the listenee. Doves and hawks may never "reach" one another. In an organization union and management may scream at one another and never achieve rapport. Disagreements may sharpen. Language becomes divisive rather than integrative. In such cases, authorities believe, the problem may lie with the listener, the speaker, or both. But something is wrong.

Also true: Even with engagement it may be impossible to obtain accurate readings of a speaker's interior thoughts and emotions, of his real meanings. But in most organizational situations, unless the speaker suffers abnormally from some disequilibrium, it can be done. The goal is to limn in the details of the speaker's situation; he speaks from that situation and cannot escape it; the listener has the basic task of trying to understand it. To move toward this goal three generally accepted rubrics are pertinent:

1. Set the speaker or speakers at ease.
2. If the reason for the communication effort is unclear, explain it.
3. Start with questions, usually broad ones, to make it clear you are receptive.

The Fragile Shell

We have indicated that engagement can be a fragile construct. The president who convinced the chemist he should stay on his job could have effectively terminated their interview at any of a number of points. He could brusquely have told the chemist, "I don't have time for that." His tone might have told the chemist the same thing, though he might only have used one word: "Oh?" Or he could have said, "What's on your mind?"

Later, when the chemist gave his true reasons for wanting to leave, the president might have lost his man with a few other ill-chosen words. For example, he could have said, "Aren't you taking this too seriously?"

But the president listened carefully, sincerely. He meticulously rationed his words, and allowed the other to talk. In solution the president offered nothing beyond the fact that he would "talk to Stoneman." But then he did talk to Stoneman. He also listened to Stoneman, knowing that the vice-president, like the chemist, had the company's good at heart. The president in both cases built engagement out of concentration.

Extracting meanings Engagement is essential to good listening because it enables facts and truths to emerge most readily. The chemist comes upon his real reasons for wanting to leave his job. At a staff meeting the participants get to the "meat" of the discussion quickly, and stay there. In union negotiations management does not raise the barrier of its own intransigence but keeps the communication process a two-way street. The channels remain open.

How does the manager get to those meanings and truths in other cases where they may be of importance? Basically, he looks for what is *meant,* not said. He tries to "get the message straight," whether it lies on the surface or beneath it. In building understanding of the other's situation, he listens for "what the other cannot say or finds it hard to say." The manager proceeds from several departure points:

- He recalls what he found when he examined his own heart: layered, laminated levels of motivation, emotion, and thought that influence what he does, what he says, and how he explains his actions to himself.
- He transfers that self-understanding to others, remembering that they too are human and therefore complex and difficult, even to themselves.
- He takes nothing for granted while listening and very little as final or perfect while seeking knowledge through listening.
- He keeps in mind that the other or others are listening to themselves while they talk, pursuing their own truth or originality, and changing or learning as they go.
- He may encourage the other or others to look at a problem differently, both to test the accuracy of their first interpretation and to obtain a fresher, perhaps clearer, view.

The listener thus gains in understanding as the other does, as engagement becomes deeper. A subordinate coolly discussing the planned reorganization was suddenly seen by one manager to be repressing fear of what would happen to *him* when the reorganization went through. The Boss may, in mentioning that "We need more communication around here," be found through engaged listening to mean that he was not told before a staff meeting of your plans to test a new research program.

Roethlisberger cites an example of how the "hidden agenda" behind another's words may be arrived at by expert listening.

> If a person tells me . . . that his desk is too small, I do not try to convince him that the size of his desk is sufficient for his purposes; I am thinking of the social setting in which desks appear in his work situation. What human relationship does the desk symbolize for him? It may be that in his organization the higher in the business structure the person goes, the bigger the desk becomes. It may be that the person who is talking to me is a college man with a burning desire to succeed. He may be indulging in a little wishful thinking; by getting a bigger desk he may think he is elevating himself in the company. When he complains that the desk is too small, he may really be telling me about his dissatisfaction with his advancement in the company. If so, I get him to talk about that. . . .[1]

No one, in short, speaks out of a vacuum. His words emerge from a maze of opinions, emotions, attitudes, sentiments. When a woman worker complains, "They ought to clean up the lavatories," she may be saying that she is used to better things, that the company is negligent in many ways having to do with creature comforts, or that she is about to vote for a union. She may be saying that she nearly tripped and fell in a puddle of water on the lavatory floor.

> In an actual case the newly appointed office manager described his new job enthusiastically to a visitor. The visitor noted that the manager spoke quickly, nervously as he told how he planned to make the office operation as efficient as the manufacturing side. The visitor, listening, became aware that the new man wished he had not gotten the office manager's job; he had been an assistant department manager in the line organization and wished he were still "out there."

Engagement gives the listener the opportunity to listen for the hidden agenda. Engagement also invites the speaker freely to reveal his own mind, whether he understands that this is the intent of the listener or not: whether, in fact, he was actually "hiding" or holding back anything initially, consciously or not. Fear disappears; the personal and true may often be

---

[1] F. J. Roethlisberger, *Management and Morale*, 11th printing, Harvard University Press, Cambridge, Mass., 1955, p. 96.

communicated even if it sounds petty, irrational, overemotional, or hypercritical.

Facts and feelings The listener also exerts effort while listening to separate facts from feelings. The two, both of them types of information, then contribute in proper proportion to the listener's understanding, final analysis, and decision making.

In listening for facts the listener may summarize in his mind. "What are the key points of what is being said?" he asks himself. He may list them mentally. He may or may not receive help from the speaker; in casual conversation a speaker will not usually label each point, or identify it. So the work of sorting and classifying falls to the listener. He may employ a "facts versus principles" technique of classifying, *a la* Nichols-Stevens, especially if he is taking written notes. Many executives make after-the-fact notes in the wake of an important conversation, often leaving room for facts, principles, new ideas, suggestions, sentiments. Other listeners will devise their own methods.

Just as importantly, the listener strives to identify the theme of what is being said: its gist. He may note that a speaker repeatedly uses a phrase, or a word, placing it each time in a different context. That word may be the code identification of the theme. The new office manager kept talking of the "line organization" and thus gave the listener the key to his real desire to get back to the line operation. The company president complaining about "lack of communication around here" referred to "preparing for meetings" and "keeping everyone up to date without waiting for meetings."

Engagement that involves close attention to what is being said and not said also helps the listener perceive the feelings behind, or buried inside, a speaker's words. Here, as Dr. Norman B. Sigband notes, the listener *must* take into account the speaker's situation: his job, his education, his pay level, his ambitions, or his lack of same. The listener also tries to read accurately what the other really means by his words.

"When a slow, easy-going man says, 'We must get on this

job right away,' you interpret 'right away' as 'in a week or two.' When an employee you know to be conscientious and slow to give praise calls another a 'hard worker,' your connotation probably will be very similar to his," [2] writes Dr. Sigband. Your assessment of his feeling may be that he wants with some urgency to get the job done but cannot put off other work lined up ahead of it.

Some other common situations:

■ A worker complained that "we never hear anything but the bad things around here—never a word of recognition." A listener-manager realized after only a brief additional exchange that the worker had recently been reprimanded by a supervisor for doing a job poorly and that he was still resentful.

■ In a staff meeting a department manager eagerly discussed another unit's problems. A listening executive soon noted that the manager was taking the group's time in the hope that he would find solutions to his own department's problems.

■ An executive told a colleague at great length that he felt the company was spending entirely too much money on community action programs, including some in a city ghetto. The executive, it became clear, was expressing a deeply racist attitude. His arguments appeared to be purely economic; in actual fact his racist feeling behind his words determined his approach. Because his views ran counter to those of his firm, he could not express them in their true terms.

Engaged listening makes possible perceptive listening, and that requires keyed physical senses as well as a keyed mind. A worker says, "I don't care who they promote, but they shouldn't go looking for eight balls." What a listener found that he meant: "I have been eligible for promotion for a long time and it's about time I got it." This employee used gestures that were too airy; yet, his feeling on the subject of promotion was obviously intense. I once watched a man run his index

---

[2] Dr. Norman B. Sigband, "Listen to What You Can't Hear," *Nation's Business,* June, 1969, p. 72.

finger back and forth across his nostrils while making such a statement. This gesture gave him the appearance, almost, of a child crying.

"If his words say, 'Well, it really isn't very important to me anyway,' but his posture is stiff, his knuckles white, his eyes hopeful and his forehead glistening with perspiration, you had better hear the nonverbal message . . . ,"[3] Dr. Sigband points out.

The visible man at work So the physical or nonverbal "speaks" just as does the voice. The tone of voice may be highly suggestive of a hidden meaning. A bit of bravado may be delivered in a whine; a plea for help may have the ring of defiance, and often does. But movements and gestures also "talk."

This is kinesics, the study of nonverbal communication, the "whole lexicon of movements, shrugs, gestures, facial expressions, and signs." Observers have estimated that kinesics accounts for half or more of all communications among people. When humorist Corey Ford propounded his comic, yet kinesically sound, "three-way auditory attitude," he was demonstrating full awareness of this type of communication. Ford's "attitude" required that the nonlistener feign attention by propping his left cheek in the palm of his left hand and putting his left elbow on the table.

The method has served generations of managers and executives in meetings as well as husbands bored with their wives' conversation. But the technique has not produced engagement —or any more than the comic semblance of listening.

The good listener practices to become aware of the immense wealth of significance in a gesture, a movement. A panorama of human emotions, needs, ambitions, drives, and sensations spreads out before that listening manager who has trained himself to be aware of such meanings.

A second dividend accrues to the listener who can read the signs of nonverbal communication. He becomes aware of what he himself is communicating with his movements, his gestures,

[3] *Ibid.*

the shake of the head, the interlocked fingers, even the set of his jaw that moves muscles in his temple. And because he has such awareness, he gears his nonverbal communication to facilitate the listening exercise.

> Brooks, manager of the branch plant of a chemical company, conducts meetings well. He sits back, his mien relaxed but attentive. He holds a pencil at both ends: a sign that he is prepared to take notes and that even his hands are concentrating. He frees a hand now and then to gesture, to bring the entire group into the discussion or, humorously, to catch the rain of ideas that he is trying to elicit. He may lean forward to make a point.
>
> Brooks's eyes "listen" as well as his ears. He watches each speaker while that man is talking. When Brooks himself speaks, he addresses himself either to one man or several, focusing on one or allowing his eyes to range over the whole group. To the extent that he is reading the kinesic signs, he is "listening" with his mind while speaking.

Brooks listened with his mind and body. He kept his people engaged. He listened so concentratedly that he could leave part of his mind free, while he himself spoke, to assess the movements and gestures of the other participants. He paused now and then to take overt account of the signs: "Do I detect some doubt—?" Or: "You had a point to make—?"

The "third ear" Brooks was not unique. He was only expert. He brought one other skill to his meetings—what has been called "listening with the third ear."[4] The phrase is Theodor Reik's, and it most accurately describes the mental process that a manager should employ as he listens.

Inside Brooks's head, sorting, classifying, eliminating, combining and recombining, assessing imponderables, perceiving between the lines of what was being said and *done*, functioned an analytical mind that worked continually to impart deeper understanding. Brooks used it freely on both facts and feelings

---

[4] Theodor Reik, *Listening with the Third Ear*, Farrar, Straus & Giroux, Inc., Book Publishers, New York, 1964.

as well as on impressions, subsurface indications of group and individual mood, possible new avenues of exploration in the discussion.

Psychiatrist Reik suggests how the third ear comes into play. Fundamentally, he notes, a central core of the mind is allowed to "float free" so that it can range from conscious to subconscious and back, pulling together pertinent evidence and suggesting innovative additions to what is already known. The listener is bound neither by what he has experienced or knows nor by what he is learning from another—at least not entirely. Thus room is left for creativity, for analysis.

As Reik also notes, engagement or rapport sets the scene for such third-ear listening. Engagement, resting on the solid foundation of mutual interest and concentration, places the listener and listenee in mind-to-mind coordination. Thus the problems listed by de Mare as facing the manager trying to listen well become manageable. Among those problems:

- Important messages or points may have to be winnowed from unimportant.
- The speaker and listener may have different backgrounds and frames of reference, and the listener may want to take these into account.
- The speaker's message may have connotative meanings as well as denotative, and both types may be important enough to require consideration.
- Another message may be latent in addition to literal messages or meanings, and these, such as irony or sarcasm, may give the message an entirely new significance.
- The context in which a message is delivered may give it new or revised meaning.
- Words or ideas may have to be tested or weighed against group or individual norms or values, biases, and ambitions.

Is third-ear listening rare in business and industry? Not as rare as might be thought. Most managers practice it to greater or less extent when listening to their superiors. Many employ it in reference to their equals and subordinates. One manager, after hearing a foreman make an impassioned plea for the assignment of group leaders in his department, said after the foreman had left: "You know, Pete just doesn't want to get close to his people. Those group leaders would be a buffer between him and the production people." Pete had made his pitch entirely on the basis of increased operating efficiency.

In another case an executive was discussing with his superior the plans for a proposed new plant. "You take care of all the details," said the president, apparently in total agreement. When he had left the executive said, "You know, the Old Boy doesn't want to go ahead with this plan. I can tell by the way he says, 'You go ahead with it.' Now I have to find out why he doesn't want it—and tell him."

Third-ear listening sometimes appears intuitive, and of course it utilizes intuition. But it reasons as well, both inductively and deductively. A practiced third-ear listener can deduce from specific to general and move as easily to the inductive method.

The pattern hunt and group phenomena A veteran interviewer-consultant notes:

> I've found that in an organization it's the rare man who speaks exclusively for himself. When he voices rational thoughts and sentiments he is normally speaking with and for others. I try to find out to what degree the man's thoughts are shared—to what extent their intensity of feeling, or lack of it, is typical in the organization. This gives me depth data on the group's needs, its fears, its prevailing winds of thought and emotion. The "group" may be a small work unit, a department, the entire organization, the union membership or some other.

Roethlisberger, speaking on the same subject, adds:

> This worker is not an isolated individual. He has relations with other people. He is part of a social system called the factory. He is part of a smaller social system called the department. He is part of a still smaller social system called the work group. . . . It may be that in the small work group this employee is an informal leader. I shall not be able to understand the feelings and sentiments expressed until I find the context to which they refer.[5]

[5] Roethlisberger, *op. cit.*, p. 94–95.

In these comments we come upon another key role of engaged, third-ear listening. It enables the listener to relate the individual to the groups or environments from which he comes, within which he works, and to which he owes any degree of loyalty.

William F. Whyte lists three ways in which the listener discharges this fundamental role. Whyte spoke of the approach a consultant might consider in an organizational setting, but the points are instructive as well for the manager-listener.

First, Whyte notes, you have a choice between *moral judgment and explanation.* In assimilating facts, in probing problems with others, you can allow yourself to be influenced toward moral judgment or toward clarification, explanation, fuller understanding. "We expected the hotelmen to look at human problems in moral terms. If something went wrong, their question would be: Who is to blame? Instead, we would be seeking to explain human events, to discover the pattern in them."

Second, in listening you can find the answers to problems *in the individual or in the group.* "In a society which places a great emphasis upon individualism, we expected the hotelmen to seek their explanations of problems through examining the personality and character of particular individuals. . . . We recognized that many of the human problems we would study would more profitably be viewed as group phenomena. That is, the individuals had their place in a social system. . . . We had a pattern of behavior to observe and explain."

Third, you can view phenomena as having either *a cause-effect relationship or a relationship of mutual dependence.* "I had noted within management a common tendency to think in rather simple cause-effect terms, at least in the field of human problems. If something went wrong, the 'cause' had to be found, and causes tended to be sought right in the immediate situation. As a corollary to this, a given management action was expected to have an effect only in the immediate situation. . . . We had found management people constantly being surprised at the unintended consequences of their actions. . . . Mutual dependence means that a change introduced at one point in the system will give rise to changes in other parts of the system." [6]

In brief, the manager should, in third-ear listening, be plugged into the other voices, other sources, other relationships that bear upon what the speaker is saying. He seeks patterns and group phenomena in order to be able to deal more effectively with the general situation as well as the specific one described by the speaker. He has action and solution in mind at all times as well as understanding.

The Literatore of management is full of examples of positive, creative action at whose core lay this kind of listening.

The story has been told of how Eastern Air Lines used a listening approach to meet a difficult challenge. The airline competes with several other airlines on two of the most heavily traveled routes in the country—between Washington and New York and New York and Boston. At a time when no amount of advertising seemed to be giving any of the lines an advantage, as far as total passenger traffic over these routes was concerned, Eastern went seeking another solution.

A major study of passenger opinion was undertaken. The study showed that many passengers were irritated with long delays at ticket counters and waiting room check-in stands. How to eliminate these delays? This appeared to hold the key to the situation.

Weighing the survey findings, Eastern finally hit upon the method: the Air Shuttle, now a well known and highly attractive feature of East Coast air travel. Under the Air Shuttle system, planes leave hourly on a regular schedule to make the trips between Boston and New York and New York and Washington. The passenger has no reservations to make and little waiting. He simply pulls a ticket from an automatic machine and boards the plane. He pays his fare on the plane.

Right or wrong, opinions are facts Third-ear listening must take into account the widely recognized reality that opinions, right

[6] William F. Whyte and others, *Action Research for Management*, The Dorsey Press and Richard D. Irwin, Inc., Homewood, Ill., 1964, pp. 10–11.

or wrong, are facts. At the least they are opinion-facts. We have to refer back to the Hawthorne studies to find the early industrial evidence for this finding.

The Hawthorne researchers began with the idea that morale and work performance will improve if working conditions are improved. They set out to prove their thesis by showing the relationship between environmental improvements and performance. Working with control groups, they made changes such as the installation of better lighting. They enjoyed some initial success. Performance did improve. They ended, however, by throwing out entirely the original premises on which the experiments were conducted. One reason: in another control group and area, where the lighting remained constant, *performance also improved.*

"What happened was that in the very process of setting the conditions for the test—a so-called 'controlled experiment'—the experimenters had completely altered the social situation of the room," writes Roethlisberger in *Management and Morale.* "Inadvertently a change had been introduced which was far more important than the planned experimental innovations. . . . What all their experiments had dramatically and conclusively demonstrated was the importance of employee attitudes and sentiments. . . . The responses of workers to what was happening about them were dependent upon the significance these events had for them. . . ."[7]

At that point the Hawthorne experimenters had to face the fact that they were proceeding down a false trail. They were unable to establish direct relationships between work environment and morale. Why? *Because work performance continued to improve even when the environmental changes not only did not benefit the workers but made the work more difficult: even when there were no environmental changes.*

The experimenters faced the dilemma. "What the experimenters now wanted to know was how a person felt, what his intimate thinking, reflections and preoccupations were, and what he liked and disliked about his work environment. In

---

[7] Roethlisberger, *op. cit.*, pp. 14–15.

short, what did the whole blooming business—his job, his supervision, his working conditions, mean to him?"[8]

The experimenters turned to a study of interviewing or *listening*. Engaged, third-ear listening was born as a developable skill. It became the tool for ascertaining workers' thoughts, their likes and dislikes, their reactions: what Roethlisberger calls *sentiments*. The experimenters recognized the industrial truth of what Shakespeare had said: "Thinking makes it so." As McGregor said many years later, "Feelings are facts!"

The feelings of employees, managers at every level and executives may, in sum, be the most important "facts" of a given situation. They can determine the depth of an individual's or a group's motivation. They may, if found to be erroneous or misconceived, call for new or different—and possibly corrective—managerial approaches.

How feelings demonstrate their controlling, factual content in given situations has been noted in case after case in this book and elsewhere. A strike took place because workers felt erroneously that a management negotiating team was tampering with a time-hallowed seniority system. A top executive left a corporation because he came to feel that his policies were meeting undue resistance. A foreman loses interest in his job because he feels that the company's occasional practice of hiring from the outside prejudices his own chances of advancement—whether it does or not.

> The sales manager of a major manufacturer of mobile homes was faced with a top management directive requiring daily call reports of all outside salesmen. He asked permission to test the reporting system with new salesmen only. He received the permission, conducted the test, spoke at length with the men using the report sheets, and eventually went back to top management with a heavily documented case, based on his own listening investigation, against using the reports with older salesmen. The new men had shown veiled but deep antipathy toward the system. The sales manager predicted that it would arouse much deeper feeling among established sales personnel.
>
> Top management insisted that the system be used. It was,

[8] *Ibid.*, p. 16.

and the sales manager's prediction was borne out. Sales went down despite the manager's best efforts to "sell" the system. The program finally had to be junked. It succeeded only in making accomplished liars of the salesmen.

The Trained Pencil

Note-taking, done well, puts the final sheen of professionalism on engaged listening.

You can take notes any time, any place. In a chance conversation at the water cooler a worker may mention something that you want to investigate. You make a note. Listening to a speech, you may hear many comments that have interest or pertinence, or that may call for questions, study, or investigation later. At a meeting you may fill several ruled pages in a notepad. A foreman may ask questions that require research and subsequent answer.

Wherever notes are taken, they should aid listening, not cripple it. They should not distract you from your listening or they may become an end in themselves and so take a toll in missed comment or statement, in interference with mental activity, in reduced power to analyze. Since listening is mental action, maintaining that central line must be your prime concern.

Authorities generally agree that constructive note-taking serves at least four main purposes:

■ *It enhances attentiveness.* Whether the note is a mere jot, or a series of words, sentences, or symbols, good note-taking involves accurate correlation with the speaker. You are required to know what the speaker is saying to be able to transcribe it —in whatever form. Attention must be constant and deep.

■ *It makes review simple.* Notes have a future meaning and significance: they are taken for future reference. They should be taken with that factor in mind. They are not the notes of a student who will be tested, perhaps, on what he finds in his notes and thus must take them fully and in codified form, textbook style. They are *aides-memoire* and can usually be skeletal.

- *It makes learning easier.* This aspect of note-taking goes to the heart of the whole listening process. You are listening to learn. Your note-taking should assist you toward that goal. Thus you note down what rings as new, or different, or significant, or worthy of subsequent investigation, or creative, or worth passing on to someone not present, or to be discussed or questioned later.

- *On the most obvious level it makes forgetting difficult or impossible.* A worker asks you if "they" are going to do anything about the breakroom refrigerator that has broken down. A foreman mentions that a lot of his colleagues have been grumbling because merit appraisals are being made out late. A department manager mentions that a research report on a new product was due on the fifteenth. You may make three separate notes. Your follow-up may consist wholly in brief memos or phone calls to ascertain what is happening—plus, later, a memo to the person who made the comment or asked the question: a matter of seconds. But you have listened and employed notes as a means of jogging your memory.

What are the characteristics of notes that serve the above purposes? No hard and fast prescription can be drawn up, but in general such notes are:

- Brief and to the point
- Clear in the sense that their meaning comes through readily
- Classified or broken down in some simple way if their volume warrants
- Legible—easily read

Listening by pencil One other point should be made: The act of taking notes, or of making a note, can and often does prove to the other person or persons that you are interested and intend to make the information part of your thinking, to follow up on it somehow. Herein lies the real power of the trained pencil.

Professional interviewers have noted this phenomenon. Managers have commented on it. Many companies actively encourage their foremen and managers to carry notebooks for this reason. Some companies *require* that all management personnel carry pocket notebooks—and supply them.

Jotting a note says in effect, "You are telling me something —giving me information, asking a question—that must be considered, or followed up, or investigated, or remembered later." Your action produces a reaction of gratification very similar to the effect of true listening itself: you "listen by pencil." The listening exercise should be carried on in an atmosphere of trust, of course; but engaged listening itself aims to establish and is carried on best in such an atmosphere, so we are not adding a new condition. The pencil, rather, can help the listener build that atmosphere.

The trained pencil does in an obvious way what listening itself does: it makes the act of listening physical. It underscores as perhaps no other act or gesture or movement that the listener is truly engaged.

DIRECTIVITY AND NONDIRECTIVITY

Directivity and its opposite, what we may call nondirectivity, relate to the degree to which the listener participates actively in a listening exchange. In primarily directive listening, the manager or executive guides the conversation with questions and comments, keeping it on the track that he foreordained for it. Nondirectivity is the absence of directivity; the listener takes an equally active part in the conversation or meeting but does not guide it. He may limit himself to signs or short sentences such as "Go on" or "Oh." He lets the speaker or speakers "talk off the tops of their heads."

"It was finally decided," notes Roethlisberger about Hawthorne:

> . . . to adopt a new interviewing technique, which at that time was called the indirect (nondirective) approach. After the interviewer had explained the program, the employee was to be allowed to choose his own topic. As long as the employee talked spontaneously, the interviewer was to follow the employee's ideas, displaying a real interest in what the employee had to

say, and taking sufficient notes to enable him to recall the employee's various statements. While the employee continued to talk, no attempt was to be made to change the subject. The interviewer was not to interrupt or try to change the topic to one he thought more important. He was to listen attentively to anything the worker had to say about any topic and take part in the conversation only insofar as it was necessary in order to keep the employee talking. If he did ask questions, they were to be phrased in a noncommittal manner and certainly not in the form, previously used, which suggested the answers. . . . [9]

What system had been used before? A directive approach in which "each interviewer was mentally equipped with a set of questions which he expected to have answered by everyone. He was not satisfied until he had in some way solicited some comment from each employee about his supervision, working conditions and job. It . . . became clear that by this method the interviewer was recording those comments of the employee which he rather than the employee thought important. The interviewer led the conversation: the employee followed." [10]

The Hawthorne experimenters did not study nondirective listening to be able to manage better but to gain information that could be of value to managements. Yet the insights and information they gained laid the foundations for modern human relations in industry. The trail they blazed has turned into a wide modern highway that the manager or executive can now travel on his own.

No brief for one or the other We are making no brief here for either directivity or nondirectivity; done well, both rank as third-ear, engaged listening. Each may have its functions, its time, its place, its value. What is important is that you understand what each is and what purposes each can serve in the listening act. You can employ the two techniques, plus a third that we shall call directive nondirectivity, interchangeably,

[9] F. J. Roethlisberger and William J. Dickson, *Management and the Worker*, 12th printing, Harvard University Press, Cambridge, Mass., 1961 p. 203.

[10] *Ibid.*, p. 202.

suiting the usage to the occasion. You should only know which you are using when. And how.

> Larkin, vice-president of a major bank, called a meeting of his top aides to discuss one subject only: the budget for the coming year. During the meeting he questioned each man in detail concerning different aspects of the budget. He led this part of the discussion from start to finish. He was collecting information on the needs, plans, and prospects of each department; he was relating the information he obtained to the draft budget, to each department's situation, and to the company's overall picture. He steadily probed, questioned. He was employing *directivity*.
>
> When Larkin felt that he had all the basic information that he wanted, he changed the pace and his method. He threw open-end questions at the group, allowing everyone his say. The number of words and sentences he used dwindled considerably; for a while he spoke only in such a way as to encourage a meeting participant to develop an idea, or to encourage the group to contribute to the subject and bring it farther along. The subject matter changed; he allowed that and rode its tide. He was employing nondirectivity. The comments he made throw light on his technique:
>
> "How does that affect your operation, Tom?"
>
> "I wonder if we could go into this a little deeper."
>
> "Anyone else?"
>
> "Is there any possibility that we can figure that into our plans now, and not wait?"

Know them by their uses Can we now distinguish between the two types of listening on the basis of their purposes, their uses, their effects? We may not be able to list these exhaustively. But we can identify some of the main elements:

Directive listening usually seeks to:

- Elicit information, facts, data according to a schedule established by the listener or an agenda, or at the listener's pace
- Speed an exchange so as to obtain relevant material quickly
- Reason logically to a preset terminal point
- Review the points of a position, plan, or program

- Obtain comparisons of opinions or data or ideas in controlled fashion so that the listener can build a case or an argument

Nondirective listening usually seeks to:
- Transfer the burden of a discussion or conversation to another to learn in free flow his views, attitudes, ideas, feelings
- Permit the listener more easily to sit back and listen on both the conscious and subconscious levels
- Undam another's or others' creativity
- Make possible the safe release of emotions
- Allow others or another to talk through problems, air gripes, and even convince themselves, as they talk, of the rightness or wrongness of a position
- Allow conflict and disagreement to surface in an atmosphere of total receptivity and thus to encourage more uninhibited exchange and analysis

Directivity—the led conversation Listening nondirectively, a manager is much less involved in the physical process of conversing and can more readily ask himself questions: "What is this man saying?" "What does he mean, precisely?" "What is he coming to?" "Is he leaving something out, and why?"

That fact points up a problem in directive listening: Because the listener talks more, he may be forcing a response of a predeterminable type. He may be dictating what the response will be. He may be *listening less*.

> Such a (directive) method tended to put a person in a "yes" or "no" frame of mind. Instead of obtaining the employee's spontaneous and real convictions, it tended to arouse a reaction of antagonism or a stereotyped form of response. Frequently the questions themselves suggested the answers. And, moreover, the method elicited opinions upon topics which the interviewer thought to be important but which the employee might never have thought of before.[11]

Other characteristics of directive listening create other special risks and challenges. The directive listener may speak so much that he forgets to listen. He may, like the cleric in *The*

[11] *Ibid.*, pp. 202–203.

Cardinal, fall in love with his larynx, or the sound of his own voice, and become overly self-centered. He may fall into the trap of putting words into another's mouth and then mistake what comes back as true and original comment.

Are we touching on what might be regarded as fatal flaws in directive listening? No; they are merely delimiting characteristics. Whether directive or nondirective listening has *greater* value in a given situation depends on the manager's judgment and what he hopes to or must obtain from the situation.

Two more questions should be asked and answered:

1. Is directive listening really listening or does it emerge as some other form of communication—public speaking, perhaps?

It remains listening. This is true despite the fact that the listener employs the communication art of speaking to a far greater degree and for a different purpose than in nondirective listening. Note the words "degree" and "purpose." In using the directive approach you will probably be speaking more, a quantitative difference, and leading the listening exercise to a far more pronounced degree, a qualitative difference. In neither the directive nor the nondirective forms of listening, however, can the manager suspend bilateralness: the exercise must be two-way. Unless it is, it ceases to be listening as we are using that term.

2. Does directive listening have more or less validity, or utility value, than nondirective listening?

To that question we have to give a half-answer: It depends. Directive and nondirective listening have value according to the manager's own needs and to the situation in which he finds himself. Does he have to collect facts rapidly? Does he have to brief himself quickly? He may employ the directive method. Does he want to probe another's feelings and thinking, excite creativity, pierce through surface or imagined problems to real ones, learn another's *situation?* He will listen nondirectively.

Nondirectivity—invitation to listen Another case illustrates how nondirective, interpersonal listening may set the groundwork for an entire listening atmosphere in shop, plant, office, or institution.

> The president of a plastics company in the East calls his top management people together without warning from time to time. The meetings take their own course, ranging from discussion of the latest turnover figures to technical developments in the plastics field. Subjects coming under discussion may also include less "pertinent" topics such as the need for a new or different company communications format, one man's feeling that the company image is suffering because company drivers are impolite, or the state of the trade.
>
> The president participates in low key. He allows arguments. His listening remains almost totally nondirective. He says, "I learn more at these sessions than at our formal staff meetings."
>
> This executive feels, with many authorities, that *some* nondirective listening makes all other managerial listening simpler. Every one of the executives confirms the feeling. "We let our hair down at these unscheduled meetings," noted one. "We know that The Boss can listen. That makes for a general feeling that everything and everyone is important, accepted, needed."

Such cases tell us (1) that the purest form of listening is nondirective, and (2) that this form of listening helps build most firmly and lastingly the structure of mood or temper within an organization that makes good, engaged, third-ear listening possible at every level.

Why? Because the manager or executive listening nondirectively shows his total control, his full readiness to hear everything, whether it be petty gripe or million-dollar suggestion. This proof of receptivity in action is not forgotten when the manager later listens directively.

Directive nondirectivity A third alternative, as indicated, suggests itself: directive nondirectivity, or DND. This third form combines both the directive and nondirective methods—takes the best of both worlds. When using it the manager changes tracks from time to time, switching from one method to the other and back. His choices range, obviously, all across the gauge whose antipodal extremes are complete directivity—if such a thing exists outside of legal cross-examination—and complete nondirectivity. He moves, in general, in the middle zone between the two extremes.

He knows what he is doing when he directs or leads the listening exercise. He is developing an old subject or moving to a new, perhaps more productive, one. He is helping the speaker say something. He is encouraging further conversation. He is allowing his own creativity or that of the other to flower. There is really no mystery about what he is doing: in one moment he may grunt to obtain additional free-flow input from the other; in another moment he may ask a deliberately pointed question.

■ A manager listening to a group of workers allows them to introduce the subject matter. They begin to talk of the company's incentive system. Listening for a while, and listening only, he suddenly asks questions. "I wonder if there's a system that combines the best features of ours and the best features of some other plan," he says, then describes the "other plan." He has become directive purposely. He wants to bring the discussion over to a different plane.

■ The top executive of a major manufacturing firm makes it a practice to spice meetings with his own occasional deductions and estimates, always phrasing these as questions or hypotheses. In a discussion of new marketing possibilities, for example, he questions the utility value of a certain type of market research. He bases his question on the experience of another company. Then he listens intently, nondirectively.

In both cases the listener's method made him more receiver of messages than sender. But in each case he is taking part and at one point or another redirecting—going backward or forward, picking out an element of the smaller or bigger picture and pointing it up, even outlining what has been contributed so far, and in that way starting a fresh attack on the subject.

DND probably offers the typical manager-listener the most adaptable method of listening. Based in nondirectivity, it still permits a change of pace and thus permits active contribution. It does not rule out summation at the end nor, intermediately, putting the quietus on a sterile conversation. The listener's conversational contributions can remain minimal and thus do not interfere with third-ear analysis, engagement, and creation.

7
Ingredients of the Method

> Where there is much desire to learn, there will be much argument, many opinions, for opinion in good men is but knowledge in the making.
> —JOHN MILTON

"AND MANY OF US, while ostensibly listening, are inwardly preparing a statement to stun the company when we get the floor," [1] wrote Stuart Chase of a typical flaw in social listening.

It happens in business and industry. Probably few meetings take place at which it does not happen a few times. What is the manager or executive doing wrong when he jumps in to "stun the company?"

Basically, he is not minding his listening P's and Q's. He is turned inward too much to his own tangential, private purposes and not outward, where knowledge and evidence are to

---

[1] Stuart Chase, "Are You Listening?" *Reader's Digest*, December, 1962, p. 80.

be gained. "You ain't learnin' nothin' when you're talking," read a sign in President Lyndon B. Johnson's White House. The corollary: "You ain't learnin' nothin' if you're not listening when you ought to be." For listening requires attention, and its discipline can be summed up in rules and precepts.

AUTHORITIES LIGHT THE ROAD

In our search now for a more particularized, codified set of listening guideposts we can turn first to some authorities who have written on this subject. We cannot refer to them all by any means; the good, authoritative statements number too many. The few summations of the rules of listening chosen here have been included as typical.

Our own summation, finally, will represent our own effort to sort through all the analyses and give the listener a final, thought-through collation: a road map to the act of listening.

Roethlisberger on the interviewing method Roethlisberger in his *Management and Morale* and other writings took the first long step toward establishing a methodology of listening. His efforts, as we know, stemmed from the Hawthorne experiments. The rules that emerged were based on empirical observation and experimental use. The five rules he enunciated are:

1. *Listen patiently before making a judgment.*

Unless you hear the other person out, *and withhold judgment* until you have his entire "story," you may miss the point of what he has to say. Thus, the Hawthorne researchers concluded, judgment should await a full hearing.

2. *Refrain from hasty disapproval by word or conduct.*

A close corollary to rule 1, this rubric suggests that the listener (or interviewer in the case of the Hawthorne experiments) must control himself strictly, no matter what his personal opinion of what he is hearing. A movement, a gesture, a word can throw the speaker off the track and bring about loss of interest—the end of engagement. Where rule 1 refers to judgment formation, rule 2 covers display of disapproval in a physical way.

3. *Don't argue with the speaker.*

In the early days of Hawthorne, Roethlisberger notes, the interviewers had a tendency to correct the interviewees. They countered interviewees' statements that appeared to be ill-founded or completely erroneous. They found, basically, that they were cementing the interviewees in error. The new nondirective method they adopted required that they never argue but only accept: listen *nondirectively.* They wanted, and sought, full expression of the speaker's views.

4. *Don't pay attention only to the manifest content of words.*

Again we come upon the rule, "Listen through the words you are hearing to what lies beyond." And at once we have the counterpoint:

5. *Listen to what the speaker does not want to say, or cannot say without help.*[2]

What will a speaker not want to say, or be unable to say without help? We have seen examples: he may be unable to express his true motivation; he may not want to admit that he is ambitious, or resentful of his boss, or dissatisfied with his pay scale.

Roethlisberger was talking about interviewing and was sketching the heuristically determined guidelines for nondirective listening. We should remember this; the Hawthorne interviewers recognized that the more directive the listening, the greater the danger that it will cease to be genuine listening. A question or series of questions may indicate a value judgment. At the least it may take from the speaker the communications initiative and in that simple way effectively end the dialogue, or force it to become stilted, or reduce the speaker's spontaneity. But where the listener or interviewer must do more than encourage with a grunt or a nod, we may presume that he does it. He seeks clarification. He asks for repetition of a difficult

---

[2] F. J. Roethlisberger, *Management and Morale,* Harvard University Press, Cambridge, Mass., 1965, pp. 41–43.

point. He must, or his understanding even of the speaker's words may be incomplete.

The social listener Turn now from the interviewer in business and industry to the social listener and the rules that guide him. The rules for one and the other contain great similarities and some differences.

We have Nichols and Stevens to thank for the basic rubrics governing social listening. The rules appear in *Are You Listening?*, proclaimed as the first book in the English language on the subject of listening, "that fine but neglected art." In their breakdown of the essential characteristics of good social listening, the authors give us more valuable clues:

> 1. The listener thinks ahead of the talker, trying to guess what the oral discourse is leading to, what conclusions will be drawn from the words spoken at the moment.
> 2. The listener weighs the verbal evidence used by the talker to support the points that he makes.
> 3. Periodically the listener reviews the portion of the talk completed thus far—mentally reviews.
> 4. Throughout the talk, the listener "listens between the lines" in search of meaning that is not necessarily put into spoken words.[3]

Note that the authors refer here only to the intellectual processes involved in good listening. They are suggesting means of increasing concentration while listening, admittedly a difficult assignment because of the speed at which the human brain works.

> We think much faster than we talk. The average rate of speech for most Americans is around 125 words per minute. This rate is slow going for the human brain, which is made up of more than 13 billion cells and operates in such a complicated but efficient manner that it makes the great, modern digital computers seem simple-minded. People who study the brain are not in complete agreement as to how it functions when we think, but

[3] Ralph G. Nichols and Leonard A. Stevens, *Are You Listening?* McGraw-Hill Book Company, New York, 1957, p. 82.

most psychologists believe that the basic medium of thought is language. . . . And the words race through our heads at speeds much higher than 125 words per minute.[4]

Thus the difference in speed between thinking and talking poses a danger. The listening mind may outstrip the speaking mind. The listening mind moves so far ahead that it may end up on a tangent and be unable readily to reorient itself to what is being said. The listener becomes the hare that races the tortoise. Yet, the authors insist, good listeners "capitalize on an inherent advantage of thought speed, making it an asset rather than a detriment to listening."

That's the trick, in all listening. The listener can review what he has heard; he can move ahead and try to guess what is coming; he can stay even with the speaker; or he can step to the side and view the entire conversation from a long perspective. What he cannot do without reducing his listening dividends is to lose the thread: to break the connection between himself and the speaker. At that point both he and the speaker might as well be occupied elsewhere.

The ten commandments In the same year in which Nichols-Stevens wrote, 1957, Keith Davis published *The Dynamics of Organizational Behavior*. The book contained Davis's "10 Commandments for Good Listening." Short and pithy, they include:

"1. Stop talking!
   You cannot listen if you are talking.
   Polonius (Hamlet): "Give every man thine ear, but few thy voice."
2. Put the talker at ease.
   Help him feel that he is free to talk.
   This is often called a permissive environment.
3. Show him that you want to listen.
   Look and act interested. Do not read your mail while he talks.
   Listen to understand rather than to oppose.

[4] *Ibid.,* p. 78.

4. Remove distractions.
   Don't doodle, tap, or shuffle papers.
   Will it be quieter if you shut the door?
5. Empathize with him.
   Try to put yourself in his place so that you can see his point of view.
6. Be patient.
   Allow plenty of time. Do not interrupt him.
   Don't start for the door or walk away.
7. Hold your temper.
   An angry man gets the wrong meaning from words.
8. Go easy on argument and criticism.
   This puts him on the defensive. He may "clam up" or get angry.
   Do not argue: even if you win, *you lose.*
9. Ask questions.
   This encourages him and shows you are listening.
   It helps to develop points further.
10. Stop talking!
    This is first and last, because all the other commandments depend on it.
    You just can't do a good listening job while you are talking." [5]

The sense of art George de Mare, writing in 1964, takes us yet another step forward. His *Communicating for Leadership,* like the Nichols and Stevens study, discusses listening primarily as a social grace or art of high significance and distinction for "the man of affairs." Yet his guideposts too have some meaning for the manager working in the purely business context:

1. *Establish an agreeable atmosphere.*

"This means trying to put the speaker at ease," notes de Mare. "It requires in some cases that the talk be held where the speaker might feel most at home. In any case it requires an easy, relaxed manner, a show of interest both in the speaker and the subject, and the avoidance of an impression of haste and pressure." [6]

---

[5] Keith Davis, *The Dynamics of Organizational Behavior,* 3d ed., McGraw-Hill Book Company, New York, 1967, p. 334.

[6] George de Marce, *Communicating for Leadership—A Guide for Executives,* copyright © 1968, The Ronald Press Company, New York, p. 232.

In short, the *locus* and the listener-manager's manner play functional roles in setting the mood or tone. The manager should orchestrate the details of the setting when necessary—when he experiences major problems. He should, if need be, eliminate factors making for "noise"—interference of any kind. But in some cases he may find it most advantageous to accept whatever listening circumstances he finds. He may talk with a worker at a machine or with a fellow executive in the executive's own office. The listener's manner does the rest.

2. *Be prepared to hear the other person through on his own terms.*

The other's "own terms" are his own words, his frame of reference, his attitudes, his beliefs, his emotions. Listening on the other's terms makes it possible to avoid the "cognitive dissonance" of which one writer spoke. This dissonance occurs "when he (the listener) receives information in conflict with his value systems, the situation as he sees it, or another piece of information he has . . ." *and cannot accept that information as it comes to him.*

3. *Be prepared on the subject to be discussed.*

An impossible challenge? Maybe. No manager or executive can be versed in every subject that could conceivably come to his attention and require listening in the course of a day or week. Quite the contrary; he might want to listen more particularly on those subjects, or to those persons, that come to him without prior announcement. In this way he may inform himself best. Yet where a meeting is involved, or where a discussion or conversation can be sketched in advance, rule 3 holds water. Lack of preparation for a meeting, to name only one example, might spell Futility, capital F.

4. *Evaluate the speaker and make allowances for his circumstances.*

In the context of the manager's continuing job, evaluation of the "speaker" or coworkers around him might be considered a continuing challenge. Yet we can question whether it is always done best during listening, when the goal is deeper understanding (of both speaker and subject matter), or later, in the silence of a closed office. Certainly, too, quick evaluation will almost never suffice. Thorough evaluation most often requires creation of a montage of images, impressions, and facts if it is to be accurate. And even then the manager looks at his montage of another, all the bits and pieces that he has pasted together, and thinks deeply about their total import before making an assessment.

No; evaluation in depth must often wait. Evaluation of a person's momentary mood may, of course, be made almost instantaneously. As for "making allowances," we have to agree with de Mare if that means, "Take the whole man into account insofar as you are able." But are excuses necessary—for another's peccadilloes, for example? No, again. That presupposes an attitude of superciliousness that would make empathy and engagement difficult or impossible.

5. *Avoid getting mentally sidetracked when subjects are not central to the issue or touch on sore points.*

Again we have to qualify. We cannot, as listeners, always tell what may, in the speaker's mind, be "central to the issue." Also, "getting mentally sidetracked" to the real issues and facts is the whole game in nondirective listening. You want the speaker to come forward freely, to indulge what amounts almost to stream of consciousness communication. If you cannot travel this nondirective road, listen as directively as you must, remembering the risks, or terminate the conversation.

Elimination of sore points is equally foreign to nondirective listening. "Sore points" may, in fact, provide the truest and best clues to another's thinking. And who believes them to be sore? The listener or the speaker? If they are sore to the listener, then he has an emotional filter or mental block whose existence he had better recognize as a major barrier to good listening.

6. *Listen for and summarize basic ideas.*

This is excellent advice, as already noted. The manager listens for ideas and summarizes them in his mind as part of the mental processing to which he subjects another's statements.

7. *Restate the substance of what you have heard to the speaker.*[7]

---

[7] George de Mare, *Communicating for Leadership—A Guide for Executives*, copyright © 1968, The Ronald Press Company, New York, pp. 232–235.

Once more, a caveat on what could be a dangerous, demeaning practice. If the listener says, gauchely, "If I understand you, you're telling me that . . ." and proceeds to interpret, he may lose his man. He may, in rephrasing, overstress the obvious, or change the meaning.

In certain situations, of course, restatement may be called for. A meeting may require such summation and clarification. And very often, in nondirective listening, the listener may elicit further discussion through the simplest of all restatements—the kind that involves merely a repetition of what the speaker has just said: "So you think our system of procurement needs some overhaul. . . ." Or: "Then you believe we ought to assign a full-time materials handler in X department. . . ."

What is to be remembered about this type of simple restatement is that it may serve at least five functions: (1) clarification, (2) encouragement of further conversation, (3) summation purely and simply, (4) correction of misunderstandings, and (5) transition to another subject or phase of the subject under discussion. Restatement should be employed when and if the speaker knows that he must accomplish one or the other of the five purposes.

THE "HOWS"—OUR BREAKDOWN

A veteran manager who knew how to listen told how, in his opinion, every important discussion or listening exercise should go. He put his finger on one other key effect of good listening: the sense that something valuable is passing between speaker and listener.

> "It's my feeling," he said, "that every time I talk to one of my men and really listen to him—not just give orders—the circuiting and recircuiting of feedback between us should evolve into a fruitful communication structure. And this is what happens most of the time, whether it's a long discussion or a short one, whether I'm listening nondirectively or directively. I don't know what to call this; it's a sensation that in talking—with

the other guy doing most of the talking, by the way—we have built something, broken new ground, created something that wasn't there before."

A public speaker might liken this manager's sensation to the feeling of empathy that he sometimes—but not always—achieves with an audience. That feeling may come hard, but it's what every speaker works toward. It has been called *circuit response*.

The listener works toward the same effect. Our own distillation of the rules of good listening that follows is designed to help him achieve it. Necessarily, in arriving at this distillation we point the listener toward the purer form of organizational listening: nondirective.

We divide our own rules of good listening into three categories as follows:

1. Those referring to the physical attitude of the listener or to the setting
2. Those referring to the listening state of mind
3. Those referring to the verbal-intellectual activity appropriate to good listening

Our Biases Show

Our breakdown will show clearly our bias toward emphasis on the verbal-intellectual activity that goes into good listening. The bias is deliberate.

Factors of physical attitude and setting

1. *Insofar as possible, listen in a setting free of noise or distraction.*

The practical purpose of this rule of good listening should be obvious. The listener wants to listen to a speaker, not to a jackhammer or a buzz of competing voices or anything else that divides his attention or distracts from the full-time job of listening. Physical noise can destroy a listening effort: it's that simple. Other distractions—the flashing of lights, for example, or clouds of smoke billowing from a stack—can make the effort difficult to the point where the effort is wasted.

2. *Show in a physical way that you are listening.*

The "do's" and "don'ts" applicable under this rule have already been alluded to at length. "Do look at the speaker." "Do assume a posture that indicates attention." And so on.

3. *Set the speaker at ease.*

Setting a speaker at ease calls for arrangement, as much as possible, of the physical and social conditions of the listening exercise so that conversation is encouraged. The speaker feels himself welcome and at home; he is comfortable. Your initial oral contact solicits relaxation and openness in conversation.

Personnel men and consultants often have their own techniques for setting a speaker at ease. A consultant notes: "In a serious listening situation I try to talk to a man in a quiet place near where he works—his office or his work station. Staying close to the area familiar to the individual or individuals helps set the stage for good listening." A personnel man adds: "I like to start a listening exercise in low key to make sure the speaker knows no one is harassing or pressuring him. So I start with something off the track and disarming—a remark about his family, a comment about the weather, something like that."

Factors relating to the listener's state of mind

1. *Listen transactionally.*

As noted earlier, this rule posits readiness to change and that guarantees that listening can be a two-way exercise in communication. The listener does not enter the exercise to sell or convince, nor does he enter it with the determination to "get around" what he expects to hear, or even knows he will hear. Instead, he takes the hardest step of all and sets his mind so as to be prepared to be convinced if and when the other, in the listener's estimate, has made a case that convinces.

2. *Be interested—genuinely interested.*

The listener must "give a damn." Without genuine interest, he is posing. He is indulging himself, or pretending, or trying to impress without making the effort to listen. He may believe he is required by business protocol to listen—and of course that happens. But in the normal case the manager should heed the words of Lydia Strong:

> Among the more damaging forms of non-listening is *pretended* listening. You may fool the speaker by nodding and grunting from time to time. But you can never fool yourself. Face the facts squarely. You either have or have not a reason for listening. If you do, and even if your reason is inescapable social pressure, listen; you'll get into difficulties if you don't. If you have no reason at all for listening, make an excuse and go away." [8]

Appropriate verbal and mental activity

1. *Think with, ahead of, and behind the speaker without losing the thread of the exchange.*

We are talking here of the art of analyzing while paying close attention. But can you pay attention without being interested? Of course. Can you be interested without paying attention? Of course. You achieve the first when your attention is feigned, or faked. You achieve the second when your interest does not, for one reason or another—your health at the moment, or the press of other work—enable you to focus your mind on what is passing. Either state is a consummation devoutly to be avoided.

2. *Withhold judgment.*

What is ruled out here is premature passage of judgment on the rightness or wrongness of an act, a belief, a statement or decision. Also ruled out: moralizing, preaching, even the type of argument that reveals bias in regard to what the speaker is saying. The listener has to withhold judgment—or any indication that might indicate judgment has been reached—until all the evidence is in.

Exceptions make every rule, of course, and that includes this one. Where a manager and a superior, equal, or subordinate have a particularly close relationship, the manager may

---

[8] Lydia Strong, "Do You Know How to Listen?" *Effective Communication on the Job*, American Management Association, New York, 1956, p. 64.

be able to preach, moralize, or argue without destroying the essential engagement necessary to listening communication. But here the relationship creates special rapport. In the average case the speaker will not enjoy preachment or argument; in both inheres, often, a powerful element of condemnation, disapproval, or contrary thinking. The speaker, according to psychiatrists, feels his self-image attacked and reacts to defend it—himself. As one authority stated, "the major barrier to mutual interpersonal communication is our very natural tendency to judge, evaluate, to approve (or disapprove) the statement of the other person or group."

A word or a gesture can "argue." It can wipe out an entire laborious effort to set the stage for listening. It is the physical expression of opposition or of judgment made prematurely.

3. *Try to see the subject from the speaker's point of view.*

Does this mean you have to listen or interview *ad nauseam* or *ad infinitum,* to lay the speaker on a figurative psychiatrist's couch and subject him to your private brand of psychotherapy? Not at all. You have the total context once you understand as completely as possible the subject and the speaker's situation in reference to it. Such knowledge may already be in the possession of the listener, or may be easily obtainable. A union leader says heatedly, "They push our people around, they're going to get grievances." To know that the union leader stands in a fundamentally political relationship to his fellow members, his constituents, may supply part of the context. Listening may quickly supply the rest. A department manager objects strenuously, and inexplicably, to a promotion for one of his men. You may have to listen—and question— closely and perhaps at length to learn his situation, his context.

4. *Listen for what is not being said, or cannot be said without difficulty.*

Looking beneath the surface or beyond the words does not mean interpreting rashly or gratuitously; it does involve an effort to reach through to true meanings, even to facts of which the speaker may be unaware. This often requires intense intellectual effort; it has been called "projective listening." The listener "projects" himself into the speaker's mind, figuratively speaking, striving constantly to keep in mind the limitations of those sound symbols we call words so as to penetrate to deeper meanings. The speaker's intentions may here lie open for closer scrutiny.

5. *Dig when you see a nugget.*

The listener is a gold miner panning for ideas, information, creativity, enlightenment—for the other's own self-induced illumination. This listener's mind's eye is constantly searching. He uses the simplest and most direct methods to dig when he sees a nugget: those sounds or signs of encouragement, those nods or questions and simple restatements that give the speaker the impetus to move forward, to take a new tack, or to probe other avenues.

6. *Use silence as a creative, positive tool.*

Silence injected by a listener into a conversation or discussion in the proper proportions gives the exercise its nondirective character. But silence is not necessarily a neutral or negative quality or characteristic. It can also have positive, creative character of its own. As Nichols and Stevens wrote:

> And then there is one important reaction that is neither visual nor oral. It is silence, of which there are several brands. There's a cold, chilling kind of silence. There's a demanding kind of silence that says, "Okay, I'm listening so try to tell me something." And there's a warm, receptive quality in some forms of silence that connotes understanding and a desire to hear more. Or silence may simply be neutral, leaving the door open for the talker to proceed. . . .[9]

The silence that leaves the door open or that actively encourages further discussion thus can become a key tool. Nichols and Stevens add: "From all such reactions of silence, gestures, words, a talker takes his bearings. If the reactions are good, they have the effect of loosening him up, of allowing him to think and talk freely. If the reactions are negative the

[9] Ralph G. Nichols and Leonard A. Stevens, *Are You Listening?* McGraw-Hill Book Company, New York, 1957, p. 37.

road is rough for the person talking. . . ." [10] The listener does not merely "stop talking"; he colors his silence with receptivity.

In this context we might also remember the words of Reik:

> . . . There are, of course, different kinds of silence; yes, there are even degrees of silence. We speak of a cold, oppressive, defiant, disapproving or condemning as well as a calming, approving, humble, excusing silence. The concept seems to unite opposite meanings, presenting itself with plus and minus signs. Compare, for instance, "silence means consent" with the rejecting silence of a lady to a man who is forward or objectionable.
>
> Silence can be conceived of as an expression of quiet sympathy or intense hate. To be silent with a person may mean that we feel quite in agreement with him or that every possibility of agreement is excluded. Talkativeness as well as reticence appear as character traits of the women whom men love. Lear disavows Cordelia, who loves and is silent, but Coriolanus returning to his wife tenderly calls her "My gracious silence." The contrast between speaking and being silent was originally not as sharp as we might think. We are reminded of the characteristic of ancient languages . . . of forming words with antithetical meanings so that only a small change later indicated a differentiation of the opposites. . . . We have to assume that silence is primal and that speaking emerged from silence as life from the inorganic, from death. If we live here on "borrowed time," all our speaking is but a fleeting interruption of the eternal silence. We have to believe with the Gospel of John that in the beginning was the Word, but before that was the great silence. Carlyle, in *On Heroes and Hero Worship*, says that speech is of time; silence is of eternity.[11]

7. *Accept emotion and sentiment.*

Emotion and sentiment are part of the real, human, organizational world of which the manager is a part. They belong in any human setting, any social grouping. They are not dirty words although, as McGregor noted, they are often regarded as such.

[10] *Ibid.*

[11] Theodor Reik, *Listening with the Third Ear*, Farrar, Straus & Giroux, Inc., Book Publishers, New York, 1964, pp. 126–127.

The essential difficulty is that the typical managerial view of emotion is highly restricted. It ignores the fact that human loyalty, enthusiasm, drive, commitment, acceptance of responsibility and self-confidence are all emotional variables. So are all the "values we hold dear." Motivation is an *emotional* force. Moreover, the evidence is growing that intellectual creativity (as well as artistic creativity) is a process involving emotional factors. . . . If a human being existed who was completely unemotional, objective, and logical, he would by definition have no *interest* in the success of any organization.[12]

Asking the listener to refuse to allow emotion and sentiment to hamper his listening indicates that he must, where possible, remain astride the listening situation and above the strife. He is not being supercilious; he keeps his independence of mind so he can think, analyze. He may, of course, have to place a damper on emotion, for example in a meeting where it promises to become destructive. Where it does not, it can contribute importantly to the manager's fund of knowledge. When emotions and feelings are running highest, precisely at that moment may the calm listener read best the speaker's context, his frame of reference. And at that moment the listening attitude is most needed if genuine two-way communication is to be established.

The subject of controlling emotions leads us out into another area: the management of conflict, a topic that has acquired so much significance in today's business and industrial context that it deserves a special word.

Listening in and through Conflict

"Conflict" means emotions, attitudes, or feelings in opposition. It includes the conflict that can arise between a union man and a manager, between two managers who may be vying for status or power or honestly disagreeing, or between a foreman and a department head whom the foreman considers a tyrant. Conflict means, in essence, divergent views or differing needs

---

[12] Douglas McGregor, *The Professional Manager*, McGraw-Hill Book Company, New York, 1967, pp. 22–23.

and aims that either emerge into the open or stay destructively submerged.

Those are the alternatives: to come out into the open or wreak destruction behind the scenes. The question is how to utilize or unleash conflict so that it contributes to problem solving and decision making. A veteran personnel man has all but perfected the art of nondirective listening—and has found in the process that it helps quiet, control, or channel conflict constructively. He describes his self-tuition this way:

> For years I went by the book. Administration this, rule on that, everything had to be done according to policy. Then one day two women workers came to me. They had a problem: each other. They were squabbling continually on an assembly line, making life difficult for the others around them.
>
> Luckily, I knew neither of them, and little about their situation. Equally luckily, I knew of no rule that covered their problem. I just sat and listened. Both talked at once at the beginning: almost shouted. Then gradually they quieted down; they talked one at a time. They suddenly ran out of things to say and looked sheepish. One said, "Well, *we'll* work it out. But we'll appreciate it if we could check back with you from time to time."
>
> Check back! I had hardly said a word. I began trying the same technique in other cases. I found that many people could talk their way through a conflict situation and come out the other side. Or they would decide that they had no great and real problem, or that it was much smaller than originally believed. Or I learned that they were rationalizing home, money, husband or wife, or other problems—taking them out on the company. In these cases I could work toward solutions of those outside problems.
>
> Aside from the listening I do in these cases, very little of major importance happens except for adjustments in the working conditions, a word there, an accommodation or change elsewhere. Listening is the key.

Conflict: spark of life Conflict is life and the spark of life when all is said and done. Listen according to the rules—and learn what conflict can teach you of the speaker or speakers; remember that it is normal and can produce creativity, innovation, inventiveness, problem resolution; and judge it not on the basis of whether it is inherently "bad" or "good" but on the basis of its end intent as far as the organization is concerned: then you have the key to both allowing and utilizing it.

For proof, consider the opposite. Do you contend that you want to "keep emotion or sentiment out of this"? You run the risk of eliminating all types of emotion, all emotion-based attitudes and motivations. Should you accomplish that monumental task, you will probably have surrounded yourself with mechanical men, yes-men or no-men but more than likely non-self-starting men. For ambition and pride of work are emotion-based just as are anger and envy. And the mild outburst of today may be preparation for a burst of creativity tomorrow.

In the subtle climate of the organization, the manager who fights emotionally for his ideas or his people may be the one who works late hours and turns in a flood of creative suggestions. The executive who speaks out heatedly at a meeting against a company policy may, if allowed to "have it out," later contrive a new policy that more adequately covers a problem situation. One company president drove his subordinates mercilessly. He had a reputation in the firm for quick, creative decisions, for alternating bursts of temper and good humor. But he could listen: he succeeded, after much effort, in establishing an atmosphere in which everyone could indulge his will to contend—within constructive limits. It was as if he eventually learned that everyone should have the freedom to engage in conflict that he himself exercised. The authorities make four basic points about such a management-induced climate:

- It offers the most effective way of tapping the creativity of the other members of the organization; other alternatives, including open suppression of differences, lead to conformity.

- Healthy relations within the team are strengthened by the working-through method while detrimental effects are minimized. Contributing freely, in conflict where necessary, the individual learns honesty and feels himself under less or no pressure to defend a position. For reasons of personal pride or ambition he can put the interests of the organization ahead of all others.

■ Individuality survives because every member of management has the right to express himself in an atmosphere of trust and mutual support. Conflict becomes the natural outgrowth of an intense effort to get a job done.

■ Destructive splintering motivations—"playing it safe," "building an empire," "worrying about your own department" and so on—are minimized. They can never be eliminated entirely, again because managers are people and people cannot shed their human characteristics. But such splintering motivations dwindle as the group's goals more and more take precedence over individual goals.

Creating such an atmosphere is enough to keep any manager on his toes. He may have to act as mediator and moderator. He must know in which direction the organization is going. He may in extreme cases have to police members of the group, and do so with tact. He must absorb feelings and emotions from those around him in order to understand their frames of reference. He must understand group, department, and sectional rivalries and conflicts. He will see that

> The very structure of an organization can be regarded as a "constitution," a constitution being defined as a previously agreed upon method of resolving conflicts which have not yet arisen.... We can go even further and argue that virtually all organizational decisions are the end product of a process of conflict resolution between the points of view of various sections and departments....
>
> The conflict resolution aspect of organizations underlines the extreme importance of what might be called the "integrative" function, especially at the top-most levels of the hierarchy. This is the function of creating an atmosphere in which there is a will to resolve conflicts.[13]

Building on conflict Conflict can now be seen to be a positive phenomenon, a usable one. The manager or executive can

---

[13] Kenneth Boulding, "A Pure Theory of Conflict Applied to Organizations," *The Frontiers of Management Psychology*, Harper & Row, Publishers, Incorporated, New York, 1964, pp. 49–50.

build on it if he understands listening and develops his own yardstick for measuring what conflict, in what circumstances, contributes to the organization's betterment, to decision making, to creativity and innovation. He will measure the usefulness or inappropriateness of conflict according to several yardsticks:

- Does the conflict come at a propitious time—is it appropriate to the occasion? To take an extreme case, two managers should never argue where they can be seen or heard by subordinates. The effect is division.

- Does the conflict center on the organization's true business, which is to perform its basic functions better, to adjust to the future more expertly, and to take actions that will help move the organization toward basic business goals? Or does it revolve around personalities or meaningless issues?

- Can those persons producing the conflict engage in it without recrimination or loss of face? Can their conflict be allowed to spend itself without serious damage to themselves or others?

- Can the conflict, if necessary, be controlled through gentle guidance, not peremptory exercise of authority? If so, it probably remains "safe," not explosive.

- Is the conflict equal on all sides, at least to the extent that every participant can make his points and arguments as fully as every other? Every man has his own view of things. The listening executive or manager gives "equal air time" to all involved in a conflict situation.

- Is the conflict of such a nature that real listening remains possible? It is the manager's responsibility to maintain the continuity of his listening efforts and not let them be undermined.

- In that context, is the conflict instructive, informative, educational—does it contribute to understanding and decision making?

- Can the conflict lead to unbiased decisions? The listening manager, in approaching conflict, or listening in general, dons the mantle of impartiality. He does his best to make decisions that favor the organization primarily—and individuals secondarily.

Remember Bill, the department manager in a steel plant? He allowed his men to "blow their minds." He understood that conflict, *cum* listening, gave him insights that he could not obtain otherwise. He never made the mistake of believing that human problems in an organization could or would be solved once and for all; on the contrary, he knew that such problems would always be with the organization because it was, essentially, people, not machines or tools or materials.

Like Bill, the listening manager faced with conflict seeks to bring it out and to cash in on it—not to bury it where it could, as McGregor suggests, wreak havoc in terms of waste and inefficiency, in petty jealousies, in submerged resentments and acts of retaliation, in any of the other phenomena that occur in organizations where the group goals play second fiddle to the goal of a superficial, highly artificial "peace."

8
Listen When — and with Whom? Closing the Circle

> People do not speak very much to one another and when they do, they do not often speak clearly or meaningfully. —G. K. SAIYIDIAN

YOU ARE DRIVING TO WORK. The radio is on, and you are half-listening to it, selectively paying attention and ignoring. The sounds bubble over you, proving out McLuhan's phrase, "The medium is the message." You aren't really listening.

You park and walk to your office. You say hello to your coworkers as you make your way along. Your secretary walks in as you're hauling yesterday's residue out of your desk. She asks whether you want that abortive call to Maine placed again this morning. She is still there when the Director of Sales calls. He wonders if you've got five minutes—in about an hour. You are answering yes when Bob Grimes of Sales sticks his head in with a question: have you had time to go over his new purchase order processing plan? From your window you see Ralph Burton, Chief of Engineering, hurrying toward the admin building. You know he's coming to see you.

At what point, and to whom, do you start your day's listening—real listening? When do you "turn on your ears?" You're a professional manager and as such you're trying to be a professional listener.

NO PART-TIME COMMUNICATING

From a practical, physical point of view, you simply can't listen all the time. The day would disappear and you would never have issued an order, made a decision. When, then, can you listen, and to whom?

The best rule is the simplest: make listening an integral part of your communications style—and then watch for occasions where in-depth listening is required or where an opportunity to gain by it is offered.

In the sense that your "watching" goes on all the time, you will be listening all the time. While you are communicating upward with superiors, laterally to peers, or downward with subordinates you will be communicating full time and your listening will be part of that communication. Your third ear can work even while you are speaking.

And what if it isn't? What if, in interpersonal communication, whether face-to-face or by telephone or otherwise, you "turn off"?

You incur risks. You may miss key data. You may overlook something that requires future elaboration or investigation. You may not "see" that the other or others are not receiving accurately. You may build an "understanding gap" similar to the credibility gap that arises in certain situations.

> You're talking . . . to a group of shop supers under you. The subject is the fleet's alarming rise in road breakdowns that have been traced to a specific group of tractors. These particular tractors were hastily rushed into service and were under-spec'd, a fact that you feel really underlies emergency repair problems. . . .

So now you just recite statistics of wasted-time and money and demand better PM (preventive maintenance). But you couch this data in written or spoken words whose *tone* clearly tells the receivers that you know the real trouble lies in the vehicles. Result? A credibility gap. . . .[1]

Draw the parallel. You feel that you can make listening—or watching with the third ear—a part-time adjunct of your interpersonal communication, not a full-time, integral part of it. You listen as the mood comes upon you. One day you "have time" for it; it works, and you learn what has been "eating" a fellow manager who has appeared distant recently. He feels, specifically, that you, as the man closest to the Big Boss, should throw your support behind the proposed new sales campaign. You study the plan in detail and it looks good. But then another day comes and listening is beyond you. You still must work; you rush in to The Boss and start a pitch in favor of the sales drive. The Boss is unreceptive, but you are not listening, not perceiving, not watching, and you miss the signs. Your pitch coming at the wrong time effectively kills the plan's chances.

Other grave risks arise when "watching-listening" or active, real listening should be part of your armament and isn't:

- You may give subordinates the impression that you listen only when it suits you and thus undermine their belief in listening as a means of communicating.

- You may suggest to subordinates that your listening, when practiced, is fundamentally dishonest or manipulative.

- You may lose the touch for recognizing when listening is needed—that awareness that comes through consistent practice.

- You may handicap your interpersonal communications skills in general by not practicing that key one, listening, as a regular thing.

It may come down to this: If good communication, including listening or what we have called watching-listening, is not

---

[1] "Basis of Communication," *Commercial Car Journal*, November, 1968, p. 109, copyright © 1968, Chilton Co.

practiced uniformly, you probably do not have a real policy of good communication.

Consistency, Universality, Impartiality

We can pinpoint the main characteristics of full-time listening without difficulty. They are three:

Consistency refers to continuity, the absence of a stopgap or sporadic character.

Universality suggests that the manager-listener should exclude no important subject.

Impartiality means that your listening extends to all members of the organization, again within the limits imposed by time availability and opportunity.

Look at them one by one.

Consistency—extending over time "To be effective a company communications program must be pursued diligently and steadily," writes one authority. He could have added: "Or it will fail to achieve believability." For this is the fate of on-again, off-again effort in the field. And what applies to company communications applies basically to individual communication.

> One multiplant company has seen its scattered plants become organized by unions one after the other. Though the company has no real antiunion animus, it senses that somehow it is failing in its labor and human relations programs because of the successful organizing campaigns. Since organization in several cases was followed soon or late by strikes rooted in deep worker dissatisfaction, the company undoubtedly read the situation correctly.
>
> A review of the company's communications practices revealed one fatal flaw. It tried *ad hoc* listening. The company made it a practice to send a labor relations expert to a plant "threatened" with organization. The expert encountered deep resentment as he tried to ferret out problems. Workers understood he was there only because of the union threat.

What other typical, on-again, off-again listening situations arise? Their names are legion. When indices of performance are worsening, one plant manager of my acquaintance refused to listen—even to communicate well—and encouraged others around him to do likewise. When a negative tide ran, he charged everyone on his management team to frenetic finger-in-the-dike effort. In so doing he compounded the misery by multiplying the problems, missing their real root causes or ignoring them exactly when they most needed attention. He changed jobs frequently. To him, listening was a sunny-day luxury.

The top administrator of a major hospital listened well when he wanted to; but because of an inborn moodiness he had whole weeks when he would hardly speak to anyone civilly, much less listen to them. His top aides tiptoed around him in fear. They did not want to touch off a new era of detachment. This executive rarely obtained anything of great value from his listening, and his administration suffered for it. His board of directors finally had to ask him to "resign."

It should not be forgotten that the communications art, like all art, must be long, enduring. Those who violate this rule do not stand still in their development of a skill at communication; in essential ways they go backward.

Why? Because all things, including individual skills such as listening, are in a state of flux. The flux must have, or be given, direction if advance and improvement are to result. Nonlistening may not result in mere lack of progress. The nonlistener may actually go backward. He may lose the ability to hear; he may teach himself "positive skill at missing most of what is said."

That ninety percent perspiration Our earlier comparison of listening to artistic endeavor has more to it than meets the casual eye. Just as the painter "paints in order to see," as R. G. Collingwood notes, so the listener listens to communicate and understand. Listening thus becomes a function of the mind as art becomes a function of the artistic eye. And just as "the whole of painting consists in an attempt on the part of the painter to force upon himself a *habit* of precise observation," so with listening.

> This progressive sharpening of vision is an infinite process; for as soon as the possibilities in one direction seem likely to be exhausted, a different line of development suggests itself. . . . The act of creation once over, the real product of this act is the continued and intensified activity, which has now reached a new phase of its development by merely having passed through the old; and the artist now wants to begin painting another picture.[2]

Both art and listening are compounded of "90 percent perspiration and 10 percent inspiration." Neither can be brought to a high peak of achievement with good intentions but sporadic application of principles. This is the nature of the beast; hard challenge demands unremitting, trained attention to theory.

All this might not be so if you intended to do everything yourself. But you cannot; as a manager, you are trying to get things done through others. You want to get things done through them five days a week, not three or four.

Blowing off steam or managing by tantrum? The story of the executive who "blew off steam" from time to time reveals another method of achieving inconsistency in listening.

> Executive vice-president Brown had been on the job about four months, "getting his feet wet," when a major program of diversification came under study. Up to this point Brown had followed the rule, "Listen first, then act." But this was not the real Brown; his natural method was to swing a sharp ax and let the chips fall where they might.
>
> With diversification came new relationships, new emphases. Whole new product lines were taken under consideration and many were added. The engineers, designers, manufacturing men, and salesmen found their status basically changed. From a position of comfortable preeminence in the company, they moved backward into a posture of uncertainty.
>
> Brown, of course, learned of the problems of the old-line engineers, salesmen, and others. He resented their reactions; he

---

[2] R. G. Collingwood, *Essays in the Philosophy of Art*, copyright © 1964 by Indiana University Press, Bloomington, 1966, p. 130. Reprinted by permission of the publisher.

could not—and felt he did not have to try to—understand the attitudes that made these men, the oldest in the company in point of service, resent the rise of younger men associated with the new product lines.

At a meeting the split between old and new came out into the open. Intending to "spank" the oldtimers, Brown spoke his piece: "If some people here haven't enough work to do, or can't get with it, I think we should make some changes." His meaning was clear.

The "old" engineers tried reasoned argument: they wanted a greater share in the diversification program; they wanted more to say about how it should be brought forward, no more. But Brown dismissed their arguments. He had had enough dissension, he said.

Now dissension really broke out—underground. Rivalries became intense. Behind-the-scenes throat cutting replaced what remained of cooperative effort. The demoralized engineers fought in fear for their jobs. Months passed in which Brown struggled to bring order out of chaos. The old engineers still had much to contribute to the design and production of what were still the company's old, basic products. The diversification program went backward while Brown sought to impart a new sense of direction. He finally had to appoint a coordinator who was able to stand above the strife, coordinate the views of all the concerned individuals and departments, and eventually do what Brown could not do because he had failed in a signal way to listen when listening was called for.

Brown's inconsistent listening reveals the danger in "blowing off steam": it may, if done without full knowledge of the facts, including the thinking of and relationships among others, seriously demotivate. The manager or executive ignores or suspends listening to get on the record with memorable, and often irreparable, emotional outbursts. He is jet-propelled, he decides in a split second. Those who can manage successfully this way are rare; they should, for best results, be extraordinarily successful so that their idiosyncratic behavior is lost in the glare of their achievements. Many of their fellow tycoons feel that even then they do more harm than good. Industrialist Clarence B. Randall, for example, has described in his *The Folklore of Management* the hyperactive executive who ranges nervously through all the departments of the company. This executive is always incandescent; he glows and flames. He issues quick orders that, often, cannot be understood. He leaves confusion and uncertainty where order reigned. Such executives at the top of an organization can cost a company its future.[3]

Top of your head—most dangerous part of your anatomy Brown's example and Randall's perpetual-motion manager show again that the top of your head may be the most dangerous part of your anatomy. From the top of your head may come too many decisions that ignore the basic premise that the first impulse or solution may not necessarily be the best one. The manager may listen full time in the sense that he gives his ear and intelligence to all those who appear at first to be able to contribute substantially to the solution of a problem. But he may listen part time in the sense that he does not investigate adequately, with due regard to opposing or alternative views.

He may then speak off the top of his head. He will resemble the blind men who came in contact with portions of an elephant's anatomy. On the basis of their differing sensations, each blind man decided that the elephant was something different. None of them deduced what it really was.

Consistency refers to continuity, and continuity leads to wholeness. Listening can't be stopgap in a temporal sense, nor half-baked, nor off the cuff, nor unadjusted to the dimensions of the problem. It can sometimes be thrown into the breach of an emergency, but then the listening impetus should be followed up. Many a company has turned to broad-gauge, top management–sanctioned listening when it suddenly became aware of deep-seated morale problems. But in most cases the listening was continued after the emergency had been overcome. In one case the manager of a plant in the East introduced a listening program involving face-to-face interviewing by a consultant. The program proved extraordinarily successful in overcoming an embittered management-union situation.

[3] Clarence B. Randall, *The Folklore of Management*, The New American Library of World Literature, New York, 1961, p. 36.

Reviewing the guidelines for such successful application of professional listening for a magazine article, the manager suggested:

- Don't go into such a program without intending to follow through.
- Make good relations with your employees your target and stick to that goal despite the inevitable twists and turns of incident and accident, of personality and problem in your plant or firm.[4]

Universality: The All-embracing

To achieve universality in listening the manager excludes no important subject. He gauges "importance" by the range of his duties and functions; within that range everything that bears basically or radically on the performance of his job has importance. The bank president who refused to "become involved" in any way in the Trust Department's work was violating the principle of universality; he would not listen even when his decisions were needed. So with the research laboratory head who could not find time for personnel problems, or the manufacturing firm's director of sales who will not admit that any other department's problems can have a bearing on top-level decisions.

Granted, time may limit listening, as already noted. It may force the listener to glide more lightly over some subjects than others. And priorities enter in. One day's challenge may lie in a particular area, leaving little time for other subjects. Many managers have noted this. "I find that there's some big thing that I have to deal with every day, and unless I do deal with it I'm really behind the eight ball," commented one.

"Tunnel listening" So what is important to the individual manager at any given point in time becomes a main concern. He faces a difficult choice, often, in selecting what is important. And the alternatives hold equal dangers. On the one hand, he

---

[4] Michael Clarke, "Creative Dialogue, New Key to Labor Peace," *Manage*, March, 1970, p. 33.

can listen exhaustively, excluding no important subject, and risk excessive input of time. On the other hand, he can rely on others to listen for him and risk missing a key subject—or a key reaction to an important subject. He should try under any circumstances to avoid "tunnel listening."

> In a case that arose in a leather plant during union-management negotiations on a new contract, management suddenly decided that its salvation in the negotiations lay in presentation of a profit-sharing plan. The plan would simply—presto change-o!—soften the hearts of the union negotiating team. Roadblocks would disappear: the company's good intentions would be proved.
>
> A profit-sharing expert appeared on the scene and worked out a beautiful plan. It went into a negotiation meeting in the hands of the chief negotiator, the director of industrial relations. It got something less than a warm welcome. "But how can you turn this down?" the IR director said. "It's a beautiful plan!" It was, the union men admitted, on the surface—but. . . . They had not talked to their people. Everyone would smell a rat.
>
> Like all secrets in plants, offices, and shops, the news went around while the union-management argument raged. The IR man's aide, touring the plant, and listening, suddenly found himself deluged with comments on the profit-sharing plan. They were largely negative: more than 80 percent. Their tenor:
>
> "What are they trying to pull off?"
>
> "It isn't the time for it—not during negotiations. There'll be plenty of time to work it out afterward."
>
> "No one knows what it involves, and won't be able to absorb it that fast."
>
> The aide reported his findings to a busy management. He got the frosted shoulder. Management had its mind made up. It would not listen, even to a good listener, on this one subject. Under union pressure it finally withdrew the profit-sharing plan. But nerves had been rubbed raw, and time had been lost. Negotiations ended in a strike.

The case of the disappearing personnel man Tunnel listening has an obverse side. An executive or manager may depend on another to listen in a given subject area and "report back"—or

up—counting only on that source in that functional area—
and encounter serious trouble.

> The president of an insurance company said he wanted to listen; but he bypassed areas usually considered important. He told his personnel man to keep top management up to date on personnel problems but not to bother anyone except in emergencies. In particular the personnel man was to report on the "state of morale" among the clerical work force.
>
> It didn't work. The personnel man reported regularly, but his reports necessarily extracted, compressed, and even glossed over the facts. The president sat regularly with the personnel man, but because he had decided that personnel matters rated as second-class subjects, he didn't really listen. He *thought* he was listening through his personnel director, but when problems were mentioned he said, simply, "Well, take care of it. That's your job." He made no decisions even where they were badly needed. The personnel man, faced with rising turnover and other problems, soon disappeared to another job. His successor lasted a year and that successor's successor lasted nine months.

Listening is part time, in brief, if you think you can do it totally through someone else, in a key area, without personal participation and the effort to understand and act where appropriate.

Impartiality Includes All

Listening, we have seen, may be part time because it exhibits time or subject gaps; it may also exhibit people gaps and qualify equally truly as part-time listening.

This third kind may be the most risk-filled. Individuals or groups may be set apart or pushed aside, not only by the manager or executive who doesn't listen to them but also by his subordinates. Cliques grow naturally in this atmosphere.

"My team"—and others stand and wait Listen to one manager talk. He refers constantly to "my team." Probe a little and find out who belongs to "my team." You may find that the team is made up of men whom the manager hired from the outside—newcomers established as an inner core of trusted aides to the disfranchisement of all others.

> Joe took over as production superintendent in a plant employing more than 5,000 people. The plant, an old one, had many problems, not the least of which was low productivity. The super was hired from the outside, was shown the challenge—and set to work.
>
> Almost at once he began to replace members of the plant's "old guard." That in itself would not necessarily have hamstrung his efforts; but in addition he stopped listening to the holdovers from the former regime. Worse, he entrusted his team members, the new staffers, with duties and assignments that went far beyond their formal organizational functions. The imported newcomers, in effect, became his "team." The survivors of the old regime began to find it hard to get in to see the super. An "old" department manager, for example, asked for a few minutes with the boss and was told, "Check that out with Mike, will you?" Mike was another department manager, a member of the new guard.
>
> As it became more and more obvious what was happening, the old guard drifted on to other jobs. The super had effectively made them unwelcome, and in that way, by not listening, gotten rid of them. The effective men among them were the first to start resigning, as so often happens.

Optimum or perfect rapport? Some questions arise for the conscientious manager or executive who wants to treat all his aides equally: what depth of rapport can be established with those various aides, with all their differences in ability, in personality, in outlook and experience? Is it possible to achieve equal listening rapport with every one of them—and if so, how? Is it sensible to make the effort to achieve such equal rapport?

Obviously, the manager's rapport with some individuals will be deeper, more meaningful, than with others. The chemistry of personalities dictates such an outcome. No two people react to a third in exactly the same way. It might even be said that no two people react and interact with one another in exactly the same way on two different occasions.

What, then? What of listening and the problem of rapport

with many persons that it poses? What one authority has called "optimum rapport" is probably the best that any manager can or should seek to achieve; the term excludes "perfect rapport," a goal that very likely can be achieved with only a few persons who cross our paths in the course of an entire lifetime.

The ideal relationship should, in brief, not be sought if it will inhibit your listening or damage your staff relations.

It is easy to see why communication becomes part time and even disruptive if conducted with only a few. It becomes exclusive and therefore favoritist. The communications umbrella should cover everyone who is physically and functionally a part of the organization. It may—possibly—exclude Manager Evans, who has announced his imminent retirement and has placed himself "in pasture." It may exclude others in similar cases. But it must on the whole be integrative. Otherwise, you may find, as so many have found, the psychological air space between you and others not on your "communications list" widening.

Special groups, special interests If an organization had only to deal with the organizationally generated interests and needs of its members, it would have a relatively easy task. It could take a simple, one-dimensional approach and proceed from there. But since an organization by its nature consists of compartments and divisions, of classes and social groups, both formal and informal, it must take into consideration group and compartment loyalties and problems in listening as in managing in general.

The challenge is essentially this: How to mesh the interests, needs, and problems of the group into those of the organization. These interests, needs, and problems cannot be checked at the receptionist's desk or at the plant gate; they come into the organization with the individual and affect deeply what he does once inside. They are part of his personality baggage.

In at least two types of cases listening has been found to provide a bridge-building, problem-solving mechanism whose efficacy has been widely hailed. Listening in these situations has created the atmosphere for conciliation for and reconciliation—for good human relations, for a true meeting of minds based on recognition of both individuality and group interests.

1. *Union-management relations*

Managerial listening, if professional, extends to union officers and members just as it extends to fellow managers and foremen. It should not extend more strongly or more sincerely to nonunion personnel than to union personnel or it takes on a part-time cast: to "hold back" on listening when you are communicating with union personnel will vitiate the effort. You can—must—qualify your listening with awareness of what the union leader as such is and must do. For example, he must seek political advantage. He must at least appear to be working for such advantage—through demands, in negotiations, through claims, in defense of the members filing grievances and so on—or he will be voted or thrown out of office. He must seek management decisions that will set precedents favorable to the union and its members.

But to attempt to listen to union officers or representatives with your mind made up, having prejudged the issues, is self-defeating. It does not even qualify as listening. You do not admit the possibility of change. In this union-management context you will, then, want to keep in mind three things that listening is not:

- It is not union-busting. To listen because you want to weaken a union adds an ulterior motive and destroys the integrity that must be the hallmark of listening under any circumstances.

- Listening cannot be viewed as a means of merely "giving a union air time," or letting union leaders "rant and rave." The listener adopting such a view downgrades the listening effort from the start and signifies that he does not expect to reach any basic truths.

- Listening should not be conceived as a way to listen to the union to the exclusion of the individual who makes up the union organization. On the contrary, listening must be regarded as a phase of interpersonal communication with any individuals or groups. The "individualness" of each union member, whether rank-and-filer or officer, remains; it may have to be balanced against the group interests and needs arising out of the individual's status in the union. But that becomes part of the normal pattern hunt.

Alexander Heron, vice president of Crown Zellerbach Corporation, expressed the idea of individualized communication well. "We cannot share information (or communicate properly with) an abstract, imaginary entity such as 'the public,' 'labor,' or 'the union,' or 'the rank and file.' We can share information with Al Adams and Bill Brown and Carl Casey and Dan Davis, who work with us and receive their income in wages which we deliver to them," Heron said.

Listening in the union context, then, is just what it is elsewhere: a way to learn, to obtain information, to find truths, to generate cooperation, to solve problems, to enable each individual to maximize his contribution. We have already seen examples: the companies in which a policy of reconciliation and open communication with a union replaced a bankrupt policy of combat and repression. The cases tell us more than the simple fact that listening, or good communication in general, can work miracles even against group psychology; it says also that management must take the initiative to listen.

Many signs indicate that more and more managements are awakening to these facts. In the fine book *The Causes of Industrial Peace under Collective Bargaining,* Charles A. Myers of Massachusetts Institute of Technology notes as one of the factors contributing to high morale and good relations: "There is widespread union-management consultation and highly developed information sharing."[5] Consultation and information sharing require good listening.

Similarly, in *The New Face of Communication* Glenn A. Bassett writes of a "feedback loop" method that is "currently popular in settling labor-management disputes." The method

---

[5] Charles A. Myers, "Conclusions and Implications," in Clinton S. Golden and Virginia D. Parker (eds.), *The Causes of Industrial Peace under Collective Bargaining,* Harper & Row, Publishers, Incorporated, New York, 1955, p. 47.

requires that every speaker "begin by summarizing the points made by the previous speaker.... In other words, no one is permitted to make his own point until he demonstrates that he has been listening to the messages from the other side of the table."

Bassett stresses what happens when parties to a discussion or dispute are thus forced to listen. "Each side discovers that it has had its transmitter turned on full blast but that its receiver has been turned off. Points of concurrence have been overlooked because they were not heard.... Differences are narrowed until, finally, only the fundamental ones stand exposed for examination by all concerned. Having been identified, they can be dealt with in some sensible, systematic, and rational way.... The bombast has been abandoned.... As soon as the disputing parties get past the stage of trying to overwhelm one another with words, they can begin communicating." [6]

2. *Race relations*

On today's troubled race scene men clutch at straws. They attempt big programs and small, and a cheap swimming pool in a crowded Negro tenement district may appear to be the Holy Grail. But to believe this is self-delusion. The real reasons, the effective solutions, lie deeper: in improved communication at every level, with all that that entails. The interpersonal level may be the most important; at least it may provide a starting point. A case could be made for the contention that our political structures, at least at many a local level, are irrelevant because they have fallen out of touch. They cannot communicate with effect either up or down. They resemble the foremen whose bosses ignore their prophecies, their needs, their problems.

Now race has invaded the factory and shop, the office and construction site. It must; the process of integration cannot really be stopped, even by those who misguidedly labor in the cause of segregation.

Against this background listening fits all the requirements.

[6] Glenn A. Bassett, *The New Face of Communication*, American Management Association, New York, 1968, pp. 125–126.

It is color-blind; it hears all, equally; it acknowledges the dignity and worth of every man, and the validity of every man's truth. With halting steps it has already started to work its wonders. An East Coast industrial laundry has for years been employing a formal listening program in its largely black work force with the aim of reconciling all the varying degrees of need, desire, and ambition on the sides of both worker and management. This firm's management believes the program has worked wonders. A Middle Western metal-stamping plant has gone to equal lengths—at least partly to make its "equal opportunity" policy a reality on the production floor.

In dozens of other factories in cities and towns across the land other farsighted managements are undertaking the same thing: upgrading listening and other communications methods to do a better job than in the past. Refusing to ride on the seat of their pants. Heeding the voices of the future in which black and white, red and yellow and brown will perhaps collaborate in the accomplishment of organizational goals before they join to achieve social goals.

Some final caveats Someone objects. "If we listen full time the way you suggest, we'll be jumping levels of command. We'll be confusing everyone with orders out of context."

Not so; not if listening is done properly. Listening should, indeed, cut across the lines of the organization chart, the personnel roster, the seniority list, the union membership rolls. But decision based in listening need not do so. Listening must be person and people and subgroup oriented all at once. But it cannot ignore organizational needs; they must remain paramount. Listening does not stop with one man's opinion, necessarily. Instead, the listener tries to get opposing views and find the real truths that lie somewhere among them. The listener also heeds some final caveats:

- He watches levels of command and gives each its due, especially when ordering action; before that, he brings in the concerned levels of command while searching for the creative solution.

- He provides for feedback to himself, even if it's the simplest kind, to make sure the solution has actually been achieved.

- Where a union or other special interest group is concerned, he remembers the problem of establishing precedents, and living with them, and is guided accordingly. Precedent often becomes as much a part of the social "constitution" of an organization as written rules, so it must be set with care.

- He does not try to force opinions or attitudes on another, remembering that the other is somehow, in some manner, a member of a subgroup within the organization and must share the attitudes and thoughts of that subgroup or be ostracized by it. The subgroup may be a small work unit; as the Hawthorne researchers found, the individual member must "go along" with the attitudes of that small work unit until management finds the creative way to change the unit's thinking.

- He does not forget to explain decisions, to try to secure the collaboration of everyone in the organization in acting on what has been decided on. In a union shop or office a course of action settled upon by agreement between management and union leaders must still be clarified for the rank and file. Where a decision to take no action is made, explanation may be most needed; the manager's reasons for the decision, if unknown, may be suspect.

Organizational histories—our whole social record of today—should have shown by now that we cannot deal with human problems and situations through the walls of compartments. Listening that is consistent, universal, and impartial avoids that major trap. It jumps walls.

CLOSING THE CIRCLE

In listening you have been building up to judgment formation and its natural child, decision, which is action. You have been building the kind of tension which, in artistic creativity, precedes realization of the artist's insight.

The release of this tension in judgment formation and action is the end product. Once you have passed this stage you will, if typical, seek the gratification of such release again and again. Life in the organization thus pursues its endless dialectic.

Judgment formation in business, commerce, government, or industry compares to insight or illumination in artistic creation, as we have seen. Both judgment formation and artistic insight are, in Haefele's words, "the answer to the problem posed, the fruit of the preparative labor, the new combination, the birth of a new idea." They are also the "prelude to proof, to verification."[7]

Hard on the heels of judgment formation comes, typically, decision, the prime mover. To make a judgment on a problem is not to make a decision; authority may falter and the manager or executive may join the ranks of the indecisive who know what they should do and fail to do it. Nor does judgment formation necessarily, in every case, call for an action decision. A decision to do nothing is nonetheless a decision. But in the normal case isolation of a problem and formation of a judgment regarding its proper solution precedes a decision on what must be done.

A final step must be added in business-industrial listening: assessment or analysis of results. In all three final stages of action—judgment formation, decision, and follow-up assessment—listening plays fundamentally the same role and is carried through in basically the same way as in the earlier stages.

Judgment Formation, Decision

The critical faculty comes into play in judgment formation and decision as a selecting, sifting, weighing agent. Its method of operation is no secret: it questions and quests continually. It operates as the listening mind operates while listening, and may use the same testing techniques. It asks all the key questions:

---

[7] John W. Haefele, *Creativity and Innovation*, copyright © 1962 by Reinhold Publishing Corporation, used by permission of Van Nostrand Rheinhold Company.

1. *About the subject:* How important is this topic or problem? Is it my problem, or my decision to make, or someone else's? How complete is my information? Have irrelevant or inconsequential side topics been brought in while the main topic was under discussion—and why? How does my information on this subject, as gained through listening, compare with or relate to other information that came in through other means? Have we accurately isolated or stated the subject or problem? What other subjects and effects relate to this one, and how?

2. *About the individuals or groups giving information:* Did they have something to gain by what they said? If so, what? Did they have something to gain because of a position in the organization, in *an* organization, because of their own needs and ambitions or for any other reason? What educational, experiential training or other background did the individuals or groups bring to the information exchange? Did that qualify them to make the statements they made—could they speak authoritatively? Did they speak on the particular subject in the past—and in what manner? Did they change their minds or opinions? If so, why? Are the reasons for the changes of mind or heart convincing?

3. *About the evidence:* Is it complete—or just adequate? Do we have supporting facts for key points, or confirmation of them? Are some facts or pieces of evidence lacking and can they be obtained? Do I understand all the evidence, all the meanings given to its components? Was the evidence logical and convincing in a given direction? Were emotions brought into its presentation? What is their meaning?

4. *About the time element:* Is this the time to decide in this particular matter? Do I face a deadline in making a decision —does The Boss require a report by noon next Tuesday, for example? Is my information up to date, out of date, new, old? Will other decisions have to be made later on the basis of what I am deciding now?

The conditions of creativity Another problem presents itself: how, when, and where best to come to a decision? Does the manager or executive stay late in his office and mull over the material he has? Does he go home and sleep on it? Does he forget it and play with his kids while it gestates in the back of his mind?

He will do what comes naturally; he will work toward creative decision under those circumstances that best suit him. He may, however, learn from the researcher, who in turn has learned to some extent from the artist. In this way, help often arrives most quickly—creative decisions emerge from conditions deliberately established. The conditions for creativity listed by Haefele rank among the best:

(1) Interest in the problem and desire to solve it.
(2) Absence of other problems crowding it out.
(3) Large store of pertinent information.
(4) Information worked over, systematic, well digested.
(5) Sense of well-being.
(6) Sense of freedom from interruption.
(7) Absence of obstacles to functioning of mind (worry, feeling that reward will not be attained, unsympathetic supervisor).
(8) Application of direct stimuli of evocation; reading, writing and so on.
(9) Provision of opportunities of quiet for emergence of insight.[8]

The cumulative effect It should be noted, finally, that decisions born out of listening have a cumulative effect. They contribute to an image that may become larger than the individual manager's mirror image. One man becomes an ogre to his subordinates because he seems to act repeatedly to their disadvantage. (Notice the word "seems": he can seem to, and therefore, in the subordinates' thinking, he does.) Another becomes a hero. Another is seen as dependable if not spectacular. By their works are they known.

Inaction has the same cumulative or image-building effect. But the image of inaction can work more damage, often, than the image of misdirected action. Action is at least action; inaction after listening means that breath was wasted, research

[8] *Ibid.*, pp. 101–102.

poured down the drain, ideas contributed for naught, meetings called in vain.

It boils down to the fact that your potential for effective efforts is expanded or shrunken by the general view within the organization of *what can emerge from communicating with you*. If your decisions drown too often in a sea of words, you are halfway to loss of influence on what goes on around you. If your decisions and the ensuing action come too late, you may achieve the same effect.

To act, to change something, to change *yourself* or your attitudes, to make an action decision is to risk failure, of course. Any effort to change presupposes that risk. But only he who never does anything never makes mistakes: a simple fact of life both within and outside the organization, one that should be taken into the reckoning in your listening and managing as in marrying or shopping for clothes. The best you can do is listen—investigate—to reduce the possibility of error.

It should also be remembered that error educates. In the absence of error, more than likely, learning either does not take place or proceeds more slowly. Judgment and skill in the use of the tools of listening will develop in direct proportion to the extent to which effort is exerted to learn from error.

Assessment—The Use of Feedback

Assessment of the results of a decision through listening is, simply, trying to clarify what the decision accomplished and what its subordinate effects were. In listening at this stage, with the rules of listening in mind, the manager-listener once again attempts to answer questions.

- What is the real effect of the action? Did it add up to the improvement or change it was supposed to be, or did it fail?

In concrete terms the questions may have a thousand implications, or applications. Did the replacement of the old lathe with a new one improve the quality of the work done? Did the plan for reducing scrap levels actually reduce them, and if so, were other factors above and beyond the plan accountable for the change?

- Was the decision implemented with a minimum of friction, backing and filling? Or did members of the organization fight it and partially foil it? Did it "take" in time? Did it show that this organization acts well or poorly?

Some inertia exists in all organizations; the listening manager, in assessing after the fact, tries to ascertain how or to what extent it has delayed implementation of his decision. The manager also recognizes that the "size" or importance of a decision determines at least partly how rapidly it can be put into effect. An order to have the Towmotor brakes fixed may be carried out almost at once. A decision to set up a comprehensive materials control or data processing program may take much longer, and may in fact be only the first in a long chain of decisions of greater or less weight.

- What other effects did the decision have, beyond the anticipated ones? Were they serious? Can we gain by understanding what they were and how they took place—and why?

The "tenpin theory" of reaction and interaction holds truth in the social organism that is the organization. Listening should proceed from awareness of this, and the listening manager should watch for subeffects of any kind. So simple a thing as placing a new lamp on a secretary's desk may induce ten other secretaries to ask for identical lamps. A decision to close a plant, on the other hand, may drastically affect output in all sister plants.

- Did the action motivate others to act on their own? Did the action fulfill an organizational need and did it in the process induce others to "climb aboard" and keep up the forward movement?

A good decision and its attendant action should do both—fulfill an organizational need and encourage others to move forward on their own. This is only to say that an effective, creative decision spurs like decisions at a lower level, either in the process of implementation or as fallout, in other areas. It can also have a similar prime-mover effect at the decider's own level: one good listening manager in a business can inspire others on his level to act creatively. The listening manager who finds that his decisions and actions are having such an effect can hone his decision-making powers and utilize them more and more freely, always remembering that he has to assess and reassess to make sure he is achieving what he seeks.

■ How have I, as a listening manager, come out of my decision—with a larger image or smaller?

Finding the answer to this question does not mean the manager is self-conscious; in a coldly practical way, the manager simply wants to know how he is being judged by others *in the light of what he does,* not in the light of what he says or how he dresses or what church he attends. The other factors may have a bearing too, but must be rated secondary to the impression the manager is making, the image he is creating by functioning as a manager.

Weigh all the factors. Go ahead again—to a new decision. Do the essential assessing again. Managerial life is a constant series of decisions and actions for the serious, listening manager. What was done yesterday can be instructional; that is the sum and substance of it. Listen to the echoes of what you did yesterday so that you will listen and decide better, more creatively tomorrow.

9
Pitfalls

> Yet sometimes I can deem you listening,
> And then all else is instantly forgot.
> —Love Sonnets of Proteus

Auren Uris said it: "There's been a lot of loose talk about listening. It's about time there was some plain talk about loose listening. There's good listening that pays off to both the heard and the hearer. There's listening that isn't worth the time it takes.

"If you don't know where to draw the line, you may find yourself drowning in a sea of words or dying in a desert of silence." [1]

In a different way, perhaps, Immanuel Kant also said it. "Chisels and hammers may suffice to work a piece of wood, but for etching we require an etcher's needle."

[1] Auren Uris, *Developing Your Executive Skills*, McGraw-Hill Book Company, New York, 1965, p. 181.

Knowing the pitfalls in listening tells us where to draw the line, how better to articulate the listening skill, a challenge that "demands application, determination, acquired knowledge."

THE FIVE DANGERS

Listening has a deceptively simple appearance. Just bend your ear toward someone and soak up what he says: that's how it looks. Seeing listening practiced by experts, some managers and executives have just dived in and tried to imitate—without giving the task the thought it needs.

> The owner of a machine and tool manufacturing firm employing some 200 persons fell into this trap. He watched a listening consultant work with groups of two to ten employees. He decided to spring into action. If it works with two or five or ten persons—for one man—why not with forty—for me?
>
> He began to call his departmental groups together. His oversimplified concept of listening and his approach doomed the effort.
>
> "I want you to tell me your problems," he said to the first group.
>
> Silence. The owner tried again. "Come on, what are your problems? There must be some problems here."
>
> More silence. The owner began to feel that his authority was being circumvented. He wanted upward communication, was ordering it; therefore, he *had* to achieve it. "Now I know things aren't that good around here," he said. "We do our best and we think it's pretty good. But we're human too. Now speak up. Some of our problems must be our fault."
>
> Finally one of the hourly workers spoke up. "Do you want our big problems or our little problems, Mr. Thomas?"
>
> Some tittering broke out. The company owner, frustrated, gave up. Yet, miracle of miracles, he later studied listening and started over—and eventually learned that "for etching we require an etcher's needle."

This case illustrates a key pitfall in listening: The shop owner went into listening with the misconception that he could plunge in without preparation, imitate the superficial aspects of another listener's technique, and force instant cooperation. He had not realized that much of listening takes place in the mind. He had only seen that "if you have listened to a person, you have already helped him." The owner had fallen into a conceptual pitfall, one of the five major dangers in listening. The five types, *seriatim:*

1. Conceptual
2. Mechanical or organizational
3. Procedural
4. Attitudinal
5. Language

The Mistaken Concept

A would-be listener risks falling into the pitfall of mistaken concept if he fails to give listening its due as an intellectual skill. He may, like the company owner in our story, take listening as a simple mechanical function requiring only a direct, forceful, feet-first approach. He may also, erroneously:

- Believe he can achieve a miracle of suddenly improved morale in his management staff, in his whole organization, or in one part of it—simply by launching into listening with determination. If listening is begun at all, it should certainly be launched with determination. But determination does not make listening an infallible, quick-working nostrum without the other essential characteristics.

- Believe he can achieve glowing results through listening without employing other means and methods of communication. He may, in short, misconceive listening as the alpha and omega of communication techniques, as the method that makes other methods unnecessary, fruitless, or extraneous. He may forget that action growing out of listening is the truest kind of response or countercommunication. "Actions speak louder than words," as we have noted in another context. In fact, words do not speak at all if actions do not match them.

- Approach listening as a means of letting another talk it out, not as *the* method of communication most demanding of honest and sincere development and use. "For the sheer act of listening may be far more persuasive than anything we might have to say—and if it's sincere listening, and not merely a condescending let-him-talk-it-out kind, we will also learn something we didn't know before."[2]

- View listening as an end in itself, not as a means of communication that has to move out of the communication stage at some point to become a management tool assisting judgment formation, decision, and action. The truth is that listening is not a substitute for managing; listening is hard work itself and can only serve as one aid to the other functional requirements of the manager's job.

We are talking here of approach, of concept. Errors in approach, of course, can be combined with other errors to form an unholy hodgepodge of misdirected listening. The company president not only looks on listening as a simple physical process; he also attempts to force confidences. The false initial concept of listening is perhaps the most dangerous pitfall, however, because it blights all that follows. Misconceive managing—view it, say, as a way to assume dictatorial powers over others—and you'll probably fail at it; the same holds for listening.

Mechanical or Organizational Pitfalls

Mechanical or organizational pitfalls are easily identified. They mark themselves by lack of coordination, follow-through, or simple physical capability for getting the listening-acting job done.

Cases illustrate what can happen.

Case 1 Top management of a conglomerate producing mainly plastics products became aware that its communications systems were inadequate. Within branch plants in particular, trouble kept springing up without warning: a strike oc-

[2] William H. Whyte, *Is Anybody Listening?* copyright © Simon and Schuster, Inc., New York, 1952, p. 28.

curred; the management staff of one plant was decimated by a wave of quits just when the plant appeared to be doing well financially; another plant suddenly experienced a sharp decline in productivity.

Corporate management went to work on communications, including listening. It made training available to plant management staffs. It created a new post, Director of Communications, to make sure all the necessary things were being done. Some changes were made, but on the whole little changed. A year after the communications program was inaugurated, a survey showed that the same crises were plaguing the branch plants as before. The Director of Communications resigned, saying, "No one is doing anything substantial in the communications area. The training has been wasted."

It was true. Corporate management had simply failed to get across its own message concerning the importance of communications. It found that it was not really controlling, or even strongly influencing, its local plant managements. Because the communications failures were accompanied by poor profit and loss records, it began a program of wholesale replacement of plant managers. The failure was correctly seen to be organizational: lack of control rather than a problem of faulty approach.

Case 2 In this instance the sales director of a national cosmetics firm dedicated an entire meeting of his district managers to upward communication. He broke the group down into seminars and launched an "Operation Big Idea," asking for suggestions from the field that could be put into effect as part of or independently of sales campaigns.

He received many ideas, a large proportion of them uniquely original and appealing. The best were developed and put out to the field as new *modus operandi*— theoretically. Checking back later, however, the director of sales found that the ideas were being almost entirely ignored. Some of them had not even been communicated in such a way as to give them the required weight and importance. A basically mechanical failure in headquarters had rendered ineffective an excellent listening program.

Case 3 Suddenly taken with the idea of listening and its value, the owner of a publishing house announced to all and sundry that "my office door is open all the time." He meant it, too. He wanted to learn to listen. He studied listening and understood its complexities.

Members of the company's management staff stayed away from his office in droves. Compounding the problem, the owner failed to change his basically one-way style of communicating at meetings, though these would have offered ideal testing grounds for genuine listening. The owner did nothing else to implement and make concrete his announced intention. By his own admission a "busy man" who could not leave his office much, he stuck to that pattern as well.

Again a basically mechanical failure—the absence of an active program to provide opportunities for face-to-face contacts, or even to utilize those that came about in the normal course of events—doomed a well-conceived, well-intentioned listening effort.

Other mechanical and organizational pitfalls that can doom a listening effort could be cited. In one plant, management averred that it wanted deeper, more constant contact with its foremen and department managers; yet management refused to install an autocall or public address system. "Telephones are enough," this stone-age management said. Yet telephones rang and rang, unanswered, on desks on the production floor when the occupants of the desks were away from them. Office girls spent hours hunting down foremen and department managers to let them know someone was trying to reach them—to listen to them in many cases.

Other companies, while proclaiming their fidelity to the principles of listening, have failed in only slightly less blatant ways to provide either the tools or the opportunities for listening.

Pitfalls of Procedure

Managers or executives falling into procedural pitfalls simply fail to go about the listening effort properly. They have an accurate conception of what is involved. They have the organization and the mechanical tools that make listening possible. But they go about it wrong. Most typically—

- They attempt to listen to the right individual at the wrong time. The effort may be made in a group meeting, to the exclusion of others in the meeting who at once become uncomfortable, decide they are wasting time, or feel ignored. I watched one manager try to sound out a union leader on a sensitive subject having to do with union-management relations while other union officers were present. The union leader had to parrot the union's "party line" or be damned as a renegade.

A choice of the wrong time, the wrong place, the wrong person, the wrong subject—all these may lead to procedural pitfalls. So may failure to answer, or participate adequately, in a listening exercise. As Keith Davis notes, likening the back and forth movement of listening to volleying in a tennis match:

> A tennis player, as he serves the ball, cannot then say to himself, "My next shot will be an overhead volley into the back court." His next shot has to depend on how his opponent returns the ball. He may have an overall strategy, but each of his shots must be conditioned by how the ball is returned.[3]

Nichols and Stevens tell of a salesman who had a "third ear" constantly at work to warn him when he was nearing a time, place, or person pitfall in listening to customers.

> The Illinois salesman . . . is a master at using the nonverbal reactions of his customers to time his persuasive sales arguments. Although he has driven across the state to see a client, the salesman may not say a word about oil to the man. "I can't

---

[3] Keith Davis, *Human Relations at Work*, McGraw-Hill Book Company, New York, 1967, p. 332.

always put my finger on what happens," says the salesman, "but I'll walk into a man's office, and before many minutes I'll sense how things are with him. He may not be quite so glad to see me as before. Perhaps he's more nervous than usual, opening mail, interrupting with phone calls, or any of a number of things. I decide fast that this is not my day, so I make a hasty exit and plan to come back when things are better." [4]

All this has to do with technique, methodology, procedure —the way a listener goes about listening. We can see why sensitivity has to rank among the key assets to good listening: the method or procedure, the way of going about listening, varies from case to case. Failures in procedure can take place inside the listener's head or outside him, in his physical attitude, movements, deportment.

The sensitive, third-ear listener picks his way through a listening exercise deftly. He does not promise action if there is a possibility that none can be produced; nor does he automatically agree with a position or statement if by doing so he will mislead. He listens whether or not the speaker is pursuing a conversational line designed to benefit himself; he listens whether or not the speaker is implying criticism of the listener. Nor does this listener play spy or confine his listening communication to those whose opinions, whose confidence, he values or welcomes. He avoids favoritism in listening as in managing. He does not go on record with a position whose mere statement will steer the speaker's subsequent remarks or suggest an approach the speaker should follow.

Pitfalls of Attitude

The mental or emotional set, the attitudes that a listener brings to his work, may also negate a listening effort.

■ One would-be listener had an innate sense of superiority, or superciliousness, that made it impossible for him to relate to blue-collar workers. He thought they were uneducated, simple folk who could be told anything. His mental set revealed

[4] Ralph G. Nichols and Leonard A. Stevens, *Are You Listening?* McGraw-Hill Book Company, New York, 1957, p. 32.

itself in his tone, in the words he used. Needless to say, he failed miserably at listening.

- Another executive who wanted to listen had organizational hangups that uniformly obtruded on his communications efforts. He felt, essentially, that he had more problems than those colleagues and coworkers to whom he tried to listen. Sometimes he said as much. Though he did not normally communicate what his problems were, his grievances clouded his thinking and emotions. He could not really listen. He confided to me once: "I can't assess what I'm hearing—not really. These people just don't know what real problems are."

Another listener may have an overly aggressive attitude, like the company president in our anecdote at the start of this chapter. An executive or manager may simply not believe in listening—and show his attitude—and fail. He would be better off not to attempt listening at all.

Attitude refers to the listener's image of himself and of his role in the organization as well as his view of those with whom he may be listening. Attitude, thus, can affect one's concept of listening itself. "These people have major problems and I'm going to find out what they are," an executive said to me once. He had the same difficulty in listening as the company president in our anecdote. His conviction that "these people" had problems that must be ferreted out made his listening a detective's investigative tool, or a method of interrogation.

A similar case is the listener who attempts to "play psychiatrist" without really being qualified for the role. The vice-president of a West Coast utility committed this basically attitudinal fault; he counted himself an amateur psychiatrist because he knew some of the more common terms used in psychiatry: words like "repression," "complex," and "neurosis." He kept trying to classify everything he heard in one or the other psychiatric category—and kept missing the mark, or making more out of simple situations than actually existed.

Reik, who coined the word "psychoanalese" for misuse or overuse of psychiatric terminology, had a word for such individuals. "There is no analytic technique," he said, "there is only sincerity." In other words, let truth and simplicity guide your hand, heart, and eye and do not let formal, stilted nomenclature inhibit or mislead you into adoption of a falsely Olympian attitude.

The advice is basic. It holds in psychoanalysis. But it holds equally in business and industrial listening.

Language Pitfalls

Any communication requires accurate, clear transmittal of message, of concepts and ideas, to be successful. The experienced listener knows or learns how to put across ideas or ask questions so that he can be understood. He avoids the pitfall of language that goes over another's head, that confuses an issue, or that is idiosyncratic to the point where only a small circle of initiates can grasp what is being said. To use too-formal language with a worker may both confuse and offend. Equally fatal may be the employment of technical terms with those who cannot understand them.

Those who trip on language exist in many organizations. An engineer I knew found it impossible to speak on the level of hourly workers. He stopped trying. A scientific researcher found himself incapable of speaking the kind of nontechnical English that could be understood even by managers. He continually fell into scientific terminology.

Reik gives us an idea of what can result when language becomes too technical. Speaking of psychoanalysts he notes: "We suspect that these names (for psychological phenomena) aim less at enlightenment than at creating an impression." [5]

If it can happen among psychiatrists, how much easier to give such an impression to your organizational coworkers!

Literally hundreds of persons have written of ways to get across to coworkers and employees. "Be precise," said Paul Pigors. "Be brief. Choose words with care. Define key terms.

---

[5] Theodor Reik, *Listening with the Third Ear,* Farrar, Straus & Giroux, Inc., Book Publishers, New York, 1964, pp. 442–443.

State facts objectively. When possible, avoid abstractions." [6]

Other authors suggest that the communicator study the values of words, that he analyze his subject before speaking, that he motivate others to take in what is being said. But the strictures pertain more to speaking than to listening. For our purposes it is enough, to begin with, that the listener truly listen. The rest will follow.

How? If good listening is understanding, and it is, it will suggest or lead to adaptive response on the part of the listener. In understanding he will grasp the basic fact that the speaker is dealing from a given level of intellectual development and verbal skill. The listener will then adjust accordingly. The college professor becomes a child, semantically, when talking to his children. The highly educated person in a management position talks the language of workers when communicating with them.

The language, in brief, should be geared to the audience, the speaker-hearer. With one person it may be confusing to say "It's not feasible" rather than "We can't do it." With a group of technicians it may be an oversimplification to say "preheating is necessary with plastic molding machines" rather than: "high-frequency induction preheating is generally used in automatic molding of relatively thick sections."

Listening provides the clues to understanding not only of an individual's personality and general situation but also of his language capabilities.

> Whole companies have failed at the task of communicating in terms that important segments of the organization can understand. Every piece of communication may read like a legal treatise, or a Napoleonic order of the day, or a scientific study. One leather goods company in the East issued, for the use of foremen and department managers, a policy manual that contained example after example of unenforceable policies and instructions. In attempting to obtain clarification the managers

[6] Paul Pigors, "Meaning and How We Can Share It," *Effective Communication on the Job*, American Management Association, New York, 1963, pp. 38–39.

heard from the personnel office the very phrases that had stumped them in the first place. They had problems with such statements as:

"Employees promoted to a higher job classification will be assigned the shift based on their seniority within the new classification."

This policy was being honored in the breach more than in the observance when the personnel man left his job to go to another company. A new personnel man took over. He listened to the department managers, saw their problems from their point of view, and as soon as possible had the offending policy statement stricken from the manual. He realized that the rule could cause chaos; it would doom many a man receiving a promotion to reassignment to another shift, with all that that entailed in terms of disruption of personal and home schedules, irritation, and greater turnover and absenteeism. But the new personnel man had to listen on the nitty-gritty level of the foremen and department managers, all of whom had come out of the ranks, to perceive this. Then he had to act.

IN SUM

Listening, it has been said, isn't just good old common sense. It takes patience, study, consistent effort, concentration. Perhaps, most of all, it requires *control*.

It should also be clear that nothing we have said in this chapter diminishes the truth or impact of the central fact that listening is the Saracen blade of communications tools. Listening proves out a truism: the more powerful the tool, the greater the need to use it correctly.

In today's organization listening may hold the key not only to getting the job done but to peaceful growth and economic success as well.

Index

Index

"Acceptingness," 47–50
Action research, 25
American Dietetic Association, 10
"Anomie," 15
Are You Listening? (Nichols and Stevens), 7*n*., 10*n*., 50*n*., 67*n*., 98*n*., 139, 149*n*., 188*n*.
Artistic creativity, 70–71
  steps in, 74
Attitudes, 57, 188–190
Authority, 13
Awareness, 80–82

Bassett, Glenn A., 171–172
"Blockbusting," 99–100
Blocks (*see* Mental blocks)
"Blowing off steam," 163
Boulding, Kenneth, 154*n*.

Brain, speed of, 163
Brainstorming, 53
Business creativity *(see* Creativity, business)

Carlyle, Thomas, 150
Chase, Stuart, 6*n*., 136
Checklists, 87–88
Circuit response, 145
Clarke, Michael, 165*n*.
Climate, organizational, 59, 64, 153–154
"Cognitive dissonance," 142
Cohen, Arthur M., 62
Collingwood, R. G., 161–162
Committees, 108–109
Communication:
  atmosphere, 106–107

195

Communication *(Cont.):*
  "authentic," 64
  cost, 7
  danger in poor, 10–13
  downward, 5–9
  as element of leadership, 17–18
  engagement in, 112–114
  four purposes of, 44
  goals of, 12, 44
  imbalance in educational system, 7
  methods, 6
  nonverbal, 119–120
    (See also Kinesics)
  one-way, 36
  part-time, 5, 158–160
    risks in, 159
  skills, 17–18, 21
  time spent in, 9–10
  transactional, 49, 62, 146
Conflict, 151–156
  yardsticks for, 155
Constitution, organizational structure as, 154, 174
Contract rejection, rate of, 7–8
Courage, need for, 60–62
Creative listening *(see* Listening, creative)
Creativity, 70–75
  artistic, 70–71
    steps in, 70, 73
  business, 73–75
    conditions of, 177
    "do's," 84–89
    encouragement of, 82–83
    steps in, 73
Critical faculty, 66–67
  questions to ask, 175–177

Davis, Keith, 140, 187
  rules of listening, 140–141

Decision making, 48–49
Decisions, 174–178
  cumulative effect, 177–178
"Deep-sensing," 111
de Mare, George, 39n., 121, 141
  rules of listening, 141–144
"Demotivation," 64
Direction, executive, 55
"Directive nondirectivity" *(see* Listening, directive; Nondirectivity in listening)
Directivity in listening, 132–133
  (See also Listening, directive)
DND *(see* Listening, directive; Nondirectivity in listening)

Education, early, 6–7
Emotion, 150–153
  control of, 90
Emotional filters, 92–94
Empathizing, 101
Engagement, 111–117, 147–148
  three steps to, 114
"Enlightened self-interest," 58
Ethical considerations, 51–52
Evaluation of speaker, 142–143
Evidence, 50
  negative, 50
Exchange, oral, 4
Executive direction, 55
"Experience," 48–49

Feedback, 28, 42–44, 173–174
"Feedback loop," 171–172
Feinberg, Samuel, 58
Filters, mental and emotional, 91–95
Fischer, Frank E., 35n., 64n.
Folklore of Management, The (Randall), 163

Ford, Corey, 119
Fortune magazine, 11
Fox, John M., 54
Frame of perception, 97

Gaps:
  credibility, 158–159
  generation, 3
  race, 3
  town and gown, 3
  understanding, 158
Gossett, John, 86–87
Group phenomena, 122, 124
Growth, 2, 17, 61

Haefele, John W., 85*n.*, 175, 177
"Hangups," 188–190
Hawthorne experiments, 45, 130, 137–138, 174
  interviewers, 129–130
  research, 125
Heron, Alexander, 171
"Hidden agenda," 115–116
Human brain (*see* Brain, speed of)
Human relations, 11, 170
Humility, role of, 49–50
Hyde, Arthur, 53
Hyperactive executive, 163–164
"Hypothesis approach," 102

Impartiality (*see* Listening, impartiality in)
Incentive, 94
Information:
  eliciting, 4
  requirements for transmission of, 93

Institute for Propaganda Analysis, 66
Involvement, 111

Job satisfaction, five touchstones of, 59
"John Syndrome," 11–12
Johnson, Lyndon B., 137
Johnston, Clement D., 52
Judgment:
  critical, 67
  formation of, 174–178
  withholding, 147–148

Kant, Emanuel, 181
Kinesics, 119–120

Language barriers, 190–191
Levels of command, 173
Likert, Rensis, 41
Listening:
  art of, 141–143
  atmosphere, 134
    (*See also* Climate, organizational)
  basic steps, 115
  characteristics of, 160
  consistency in, 161–165
  creative, 69, 78-80
    aids to, 84–89
  dangers in, 183
  defined, 4
  de Mare's rules, 141–143
  directive, 129–134
    purposes, 131–132
  distinguished from hearing, 24
  downward, 4
    (*See also* Communication, downward)

Listening *(Cont.)*:
  evaluation, 142–143
  facts or feelings, 117–119
  "facts vs. principles," 117
  feedback, 28, 42–44, 173–174
    use of, 178–180
  feed-in, 28
  full-time, 173
    caveats, 173–174
    characteristics of, 160
  goals, 25, 27, 68–69
  good, three categories of, 145
  guidelines, 84–89
  for "hidden agenda," 115–116
  impartiality in, 167–174
  importance of, 9–10
  lateral, 4
  learning, 17–18
  for meanings, 115
  misconceptions, 19, 183
  nondirective, 129–135
    purposes, 132
  part-time, 167–168
  by pencil, 128–129
  perceptive, 118
  physical preparation for, 103–109
  pretended, 147
  problems in, listed by de Mare, 121
  procedure, 187
  "projective," 148–149
  purposes, 42–43
  and sensitivity, 75
  statistics, 9–10
  technique, 24, 26–27, 140–141, 146–155
  "with the third ear," 120–122
  transactional, 146
  "tunnel," 165–167

Listening *(Cont.)*:
  universality in, 165–167
  upward, 4
  what it is not, 145
  when called for, 158–160
Listening survey, 14

McCormick, Charles, 63
McGregor, Douglas, 19, 20n., 25, 31, 41, 46n., 59, 62, 80, 126, 150–151, 156
Machaver, William V., 32n.
McLuhan, Marshall, 157
Maier, Norman F., 41n.
Management:
  goals of, 25, 31–32
  objective vs. directive, 62–63
  participative, 19, 28
  pitfalls, 10–13
  social sciences applied in, 41
  strategy, 59
  styles, 16–21, 37–39
  Theory X, 19
  Theory Y, 19, 41
  training courses, 57
  traps in, 79–80
"Managerial blindness," 16
Managers, three types of, 36–38
Manager's role, 1–3, 21
Manipulation, 103
Marrow, Alfred J., 28n.
Mayo, Elton, 41
Mechanical aids, 186
Meetings, 108–109
Mental blocks, 91–95
  identifying, 98–99
Michelangelo, 70
Mini-society, 4
"Monster in the back room," 88–89

Motivation, 28–29
  manager's, 57–59
Motivational climate, 64
  (*See also* Climate,
  organizational)
Murphy, Denis, 8*n*.
Myers, Charles A., 171

National Industrial Conference
  Board, 7
National Labor Relations Board,
  40
Negative evidence, 50
Newcomb, Robert, 43, 76–77
Nichols, Ralph G., 10, 30, 50*n*.,
  53, 98, 117, 139, 149, 187
  rules of listening, 139
Nixon, Richard M., 91
"Noise," 142
Nondirectivity in listening,
  133–134
  (*See also* Listening,
  nondirective)
Nonleadership, 14–16
Nonlistening, 6, 39-41, 161
  as cause of nonleadership,
  14–16
  effects of, 10–14
Nonverbal communication,
  119–120
  (*See also* Kinesics)
Nonverbal messages, 118–119
Nonverbal reactions, 187–188
Note-taking, 127–129
  characteristics of, 128
  notebooks for, 128–129

Odiorne, George S., 9, 55

"Old brain," 85
One-way pitch, 31
Operational efficacy, 2
Opinion Research Corporation,
  16, 44
Organizational goals, 33–35
Osborn, Alex F., 87–88

Paragon, P. J., 76
Participation, limits of, 28
Part-time communication (*see*
  Communication, part-time)
Patience, 56–57
Penney, J. C., 10
"People approach," 65
People orientation, 66
Personality:
  group, 169
  management, 16–17
Perspective, 173–174
Physical planning for meetings,
  103–106
Pigors, Paul, 190–191
Planty, Earl G., 32*n*.
Point of view, 148
Pollak, Otto, 51
Precedent, 174
Product checklist, 88
Projective listening, 148–149
"Psychoanalese," 189

Race relations, 172–173
Randall, Clarence B., 90, 163
Rankin, Paul T., 9
Rapport, 111, 168–169
  "optimum," 169
Redfield, Charles E., 18*n*.
Reik, Theodor, 93, 120, 121, 150,
  189, 190

Restatement, function of, 144
Roethlisberger, F. J., 8, 41, 115, 116n., 122, 126–126, 129–130, 137–138
   rules for listening, 138–139

Sammons, Marg, 43, 76–77
Schmidt, Warren H., 25n.
Schwab, Charles, 22
Self-development, 17
Self-fulfilling prophecy, 62
Self-image, 101
Sense of direction, 55
Sensitivity, listening and, 75
Shakespeare, William, 126
Sigband, Norman B., 117–119
Silence, 149–150
Social listening, 139–140
Speeches, 172
Splintering motivations, 154
Steel Workers Union, 86–87
Stereotypes, 95–99
   cure of, 98–99
   kinds of, 95–98
Stevens, Leonard A., 10, 30, 50n., 53, 98, 117, 139, 149, 187
   rules of listening, 139
Stevenson, Adlai, 30
Strikes, 3, 15, 126, 166
Strong, Lydia, 147

Talking-listening conferences, 107
Tannenbaum, Robert H., 25n.
Targets in listening, 31–35

"Tenpin theory," 179
Therapy, 34
"Third ear, listening with the," 120–122
Thought patterns, 85
Thought speed, 140
   (*See also* Brain, speed of)
"Top of your head," 164–165
"Trained pencil," 129
Transactionality, 146
Transmission of information, 93
Truman, Harry S., 23
"Tunnel listening," 165–167

Understanding gap (*see* Gaps, understanding)
Union-busting, 170
Union contracts, rejection of, 7–8
Union participation, 170–171
Universality, 165–167
Unlistening, 40
   (*See also* Nonlistening)
Uris, Auren, 181

van Garrett, Wouter, 21n.
Vision, artist's, 162

"Watching-listening," 158–160
   risks, 159–160
Whyte, William Foote, 25, 36, 86–87, 123–124, 184n.
Wikstrom, Walter S., 7
Word barriers, 98